Praise for *Clergy Succession*

"Few events in the life of any organization are as important, risky, and stressful as a change of leadership. Two exceedingly effective pastors and leaders have combined to share practices out of their experience to make successful pastoral transitions far more likely. Nowhere is such work more critical than the time when a long-tenured pastor leaves a large congregation."

—Lovett H. Weems, Jr., author of *An Aura of Hope: United Methodism's Next Chapter in the United States*

"I have long believed that God moves at the speed of the relationships we build. In *Clergy Succession*, we learn how to increase the impact of saying goodbye well and how to say hello well. This resource breaks down important steps that can positively impact the future of the church, which builds upon the success of the past. I highly recommend this book."

—Scott Carlson, Director of Congregational Development, Wisconsin Annual Conference of The United Methodist Church

"*Clergy Succession* is a must-read book tailored for laity, clergy, and judicatory leaders who are navigating the intricate process of staff-led denominational church transitions. Authors Jim and Stan offer a captivating narrative of the Lovers Lane United Methodist Church Senior Pastor transition, illustrating a remarkable journey of preparation, discernment, and collaboration between the congregation and the annual conference. This meticulously planned and executed transition is a testament to the power of shared agency and mutual affirmation. *Clergy Succession* provides adaptable principles and processes, equipping readers to apply them contextually while maintaining a clear focus on the underlying 'why.'"

—Joe Park, CEO of Horizons Stewardship and Next Level Generosity

Other Abingdon Press Books by Jim Ozier

Church Culture
(co-author: Yvette Thibodeaux)

The Changeover Zone
(co-author: Jim Griffith)

Clip In
(co-author: Fiona Haworth)

Jim Ozier
with Stan Copeland

Clergy Succession

Building a Bridge to Your Church's Future

Abingdon Press
Nashville

CLERGY SUCCESSION:
BUILDING A BRIDGE TO YOUR CHURCH'S FUTURE

ISBN 978-1-7910-4240-0

Library of Congress Control Number: 2026946027

Book cover for *Clergy Succession: Building a Bridge to Your Church's Future* by Jim Ozier and Stan Copeland features a bridge extending across water beneath a golden sunrise.

MANUFACTURED IN THE UNITED STATES OF AMERICA

Contents

PART THREE
PASTORAL SEARCHES: THE CONSULTATIVE MODEL

PART FOUR
BUILDING A SUCCESSFUL TRANSITION BRIDGE

Acknowledgments

We thank all contributors to this book, including bishops, church scholars, exiting and arriving pastors, staff members, and local church leaders. We utilize many tools in our transition work. Most are summarized in this book . . . and all are referenced, detailed, and available at the Abingdon Press website.

Introduction

Jim Ozier, Church Difference Makers Founder and CEO

My father was multiply handicapped, but that didn't stop Pastor Dale Gatlin from including him in all the men's activities at my home church, Douglas Avenue UMC in Springfield, Illinois. Around our dinner table we heard many stories of Dale personally carrying my dad on his back while the guys portaged their canoes from one fishing spot to another in the backwaters of Michigan. That dad was sickly, small, and frail—having no use of his legs—meant little to our large, loud, boisterous pastor who seemed able to care for anyone at any time. He was amazing and we loved him dearly.

Dale was just another of a long procession of pastors to Douglas Ave, but to my family, pastor Dale was not just "our pastor," he was our angel of God! I was a seventh grader and had no understanding of the inner workings of the church or its politics of decision making. Perhaps other parishioners were not so keen on Dale because suddenly one Sunday morning we were shocked with the news that he would be leaving the church after the upcoming annual conference and going to serve somewhere else in central Illinois.

Even though my family was influential and instrumental in the church, we were just one family. We felt robbed of our dad's saving grace.

Our grief was almost inconsolable. I've heard it said that the root word for "bereaved" as in "bereavement," comes from the old English word for "being robbed." That's the way we felt: robbed of the preacher who made my dad with a disability feel seen.

I am not suggesting that any pastoral transition can meet the needs and the expectations of every person in a church. And no transition can be a guaranteed success—there are just too many variables. I am suggesting that we can improve the odds of having a great transition that reduces anxiety and sets the successor up for success when we (a) prepare with intentionality; (b) realize our compelling motivation is to reflect the spirit and culture of our Wesleyan heritage; and (c) proceed by seeing the transition as a growth opportunity because of our love for Jesus Christ and the desire to bring more people to him.

Every pastoral transition is a bridge to the church's future that spans from today to tomorrow, from the present to the next, from the "what is" to the "what can be." A bridge is built to get people or products from one place to another and is built to overcome natural obstacles and sometimes seemingly difficult challenges. Whether a bridge is as utilitarian as an iron railroad trestle or as quaint as an Indiana covered bridge, it is built for specific situations in light of observable needs and desires. The same is true of a pastoral transition bridge to a church's future: there is a need that can also become a hope; a challenge that can become an opportunity.

And we all know we have many challenges today. Think about it: After the season of disaffiliations, there are approximately 22,882 United Methodist (my tribe) congregations in the US. today. Each year, roughly 30–40 percent of those experience a pastoral change. That's between 6,800 and 9,100 congregations—and countless thousands of people—saying goodbye to one pastor and hello to another every year. That's a lot of transition.

But transitions are not just transactions! Done well they bring about transformation. There's a world of relationships—some of the everyday variety like that between a pastor and a parishioner; yet others of a more profound sort due to shared life experiences that bring a profound depth. The grief my family experienced when Pastor Dale left is the way some people in any pastoral transition must feel, especially if the beloved pastor has enjoyed a long tenure in which she or he has been an integral part of generations of a family: They baptized baby Sue, watched her grow up, presided at her marriage, buried her parents, and also baptized her new baby. These are pastoral connections that transcend a goodbye.

I'm sure that Pastor Dale's successor was a fine man and minister. No doubt he did a worthy job of leading the church. But I can't even remember his name. I am not blaming anyone or anything. It is just a reality of pastoral transitions—and that is why I have devoted the last ten years of my life to helping churches do transitions better by avoiding having a transition just become another ho-hum transaction, remembering and honoring the deep truth that people's feelings are often under the surface of "saying goodbye and saying hello," and helping us practice transitions as prayerful and care-full work.

Be assured that bishops and cabinets approach pastoral transitions in that spirit. When churches are building transition bridges to their future, bishops and superintendents take their responsibility seriously, prayerfully, and pastorally, partnering with each of the churches over whom they have supervisory responsibility. It is not a simple bureaucratic deployment of personnel. They are acutely aware that each church is unique in its setting, circumstances, and needs. I served on an appointment cabinet for seven years and have worked with dozens of cabinets on transition issues and have always seen this truth revealed.

Come appointment time, they know that some of their churches will be building a bridge over the wide gap of uncertainty or the deep gully of decline; some will find themselves building over the messy swamp of conflict, and others over the swirling river of demographic change; while occasionally a church finds itself building a bridge over the desert wasteland gorge of toxicity.

Every year a few churches deal with the anxiety and opportunity of building a transition bridge to span the chasm caused by the retirement of a long-tenured beloved pastor around whose personality the church finds its identity. And in many conferences transition bridges must traverse the sparse landscape of limited availability of pastors while at the same time negotiating the lingering effects of Covid and disaffiliations that still impact the church world.

Regardless of circumstances or challenges, in most transitions the UMC spirit of positivity and faithfulness is borne out in that old saying, "We are building the bridge while we are traveling on it!" It proclaims our age-old confidence and hope that in passing the baton of leadership from one pastor to the next, God's hand is at work even more than our human hands.

Our company, Church Difference Makers, exists to help bishops and cabinets in two significant ways: One is to prepare churches entering a time of transition to build strong bridges to their future; the other is to conduct a pastoral search when requested, with the bishop's blessing.

A transition, when it is not perceived as a simple transaction, brings about transformation. That transformation happens when a church—and the conference—shows out and shines because of transitions done well. It happens when everyone involved—the church, the exiting and arriving pastors, and the conference—reflects the kind of loving, courteous, sensitive culture that we aspire to have. A church has no better opportunity to grow than when a pastoral transition is done well! You can read more about this in my 2016 Abingdon book, *The Changeover Zone: Successful Pastoral Transitions*, which we reference frequently in this book.

About a third of this book is about creating a culture where we do transitions better—elevating them beyond a functional transaction into the realm of reflecting the culture of Jesus Christ in the Wesleyan spirit. Most of this book, however, is about the prior step in many pastoral transitions: **Succession Planning and Planned Successions**, which are often less understood and underappreciated. These key steps can sometimes, in partnership with the bishop, lead to promoting a church's admired and excellent associate into the role of the senior pastor, as is being done at Highland Park UMC in 2026. It can also, in specialized situations, lead to conducting a pastoral search for a local church in a clearly articulated process, again in partnership with the resident bishop. And so, we devote many pages to explaining all the nuances of finding the "right match" for a church.

The part of the book focusing on planned successions and succession planning features the Reverend Doctor Stan Copeland, longtime pastor of one of United Methodism's stellar churches, Lovers Lane UMC, in Dallas, going to his bishop, Ruben Saenz Jr., in late 2023 to share his heart about the uncertainties of when to retire. He also requested and received the bishop's permission to contract with Church Difference Makers. Stan was so intent on clarity that he even created a "Collaboration Agreement" (more about this later), which carried the signatures of Stan, the bishop, the Lovers Lane chairperson, and me as the consultant. It outlined the bishop's parameters and protocols required of the church and consultant when conducting a nationwide search for its next senior pastor.

The planned succession continued with a great executive staff at Lovers Lane who, amid uncertainty of what would happen when they lost their beloved pastor of twenty-seven years, soldiered on with courage and determination. This staff, due to the compelling and compassionate leadership of executive pastors Kay Eck, Jeff Jones, and Donna Whitehead, in conjunction with the five campus community pastors, supported a highly motivated, dedicated church-wide staff. This supportive collaboration created a positive spirit and a hopeful anticipation to overcome anxiety.

The transition plowed forward with an amazing team of laity who were intentionally formed as an extension of the Staff-Parish Relations Committee called "the succession team." This hardworking team made up of dynamic church members representing the various worshipping communities and constituencies worked cooperatively with Bishop Ruben Saenz Jr. and District Superintendent Edlen Cowley, guided by the consultative experience of the Church Difference Makers.

And it found its fulfillment with Bishop Saenz appointing Dr. Eddie Rester as Lovers Lane's next senior pastor. Eddie came from the Mississippi Conference and possessed all the experience, skills, and talents the church was looking for, as well as the heart to match Lovers Lane's culture.

Over the previous ten years I have worked with hundreds of churches going through pastoral transitions, and more than a dozen pastoral searches with the blessing of the resident bishops of those churches. But none of my previous engagements presented a better opportunity to demonstrate how to make a great transition, or a pastoral search more effectively. During the transition work with Lovers Lane, I became enamored with the church! And Stan became enamored with our work. This resulted in the two of us writing this book together, and with Stan joining Church Difference Makers as a team member and leader.

That is why we put all this together as a case study—the good and the bad—to put flesh on the bones of the principles, systems, tools, and techniques that go into a transition that builds a bridge to the church's future. Thank you to all the congregations, bishops, cabinet members, and pastors over the years without whom this book could not have happened. We are so grateful for all these dedicated bridge builders so committed to the work of the church and God's kingdom. Enjoy!

PART ONE

Successful Pastoral Transitions

Then Elisha picked up the mantle that had fallen from Elijah.
—2 Kings 2:13

Chapter 1

Becoming More Intentional About Pastoral Transitions

Jim Ozier

"I was here before that preacher came, and I'll be here after he's gone." That's what my mother used to say every time our home church in rural Illinois got a new pastor. This was back in the 1950s and 1960s, and she held true to her stance even after we moved to the big city; pastoral transitions were frequent, and I still remember her words clearly.

Today the church world has changed. My mother's brand of loyalty—anchored in staying no matter who the pastor was—isn't nearly as common. Too often, when a pastoral transition isn't handled well, people simply walk away. We can't measure how many have left our churches because of transitions done poorly, but we see the reality everywhere. Most of us have watched good church folk leave rather than face the uncertainty of what's next—or the awkwardness of a system that seemed to heighten that anxiety.

Anxiety Inherent in Pastoral Transitions

When there is a change of lead pastors, the anxiety is always greater than most bishops, district superintendents, or Staff-Parish Relations Committee chairs realize. At Church Difference Makers, we work alongside bishops, cabinets, and local churches through these transitions. Our mission is simple: to minimize anxiety and maximize excitement. We want to shift the culture from "A change of pastors? We'll get through it" to "A change of pastors? We'll grow through it!" That cultural shift matters, because few opportunities for growth are as powerful as a pastoral transition done well.

What "Done Well" Looks Like

There are transitions done poorly for sure and in hindsight we can analyze mistakes and missteps in the process, but when transition is done well, transitions benefit everyone involved, propelling the church forward. A healthy transition is marked by:

- **excitement and goodwill** as the church says both "goodbye" and "hello";
- *trust and partnership* deepened between the local church and the conference;
- **diminished anxiety** and healthy anticipation for both the congregation and the arriving pastor; and
- **hope for vitality**, rather than the fear of decline, that permeates the congregation and contributes to confidence in the cabinet.

Mark Hart, chair of the Lovers Lane Succession Team during their pastoral transition in 2025 says this about a transition done well in his written review of the process: "As chair of both our SPRC and our succession team, I had a front-row seat for our pastoral transition. I know what it looks like when done well! Working with a transition consultant was instrumental in Lovers Lane being able to successfully transition from our senior pastor of twenty-eight years in Stan Copeland to our new senior pastor Eddie Rester, who came to us from Mississippi. Church Difference Makers' experience and guiding hand proved pivotal in being able to properly say goodbye to Stan and warmly welcome Eddie. Their involvement gave us a wonderful framework to launch this new season with excitement and renewed energy. We are six months into Eddie's tenure and we couldn't be more thrilled. We have seen increased attendance, engagement, and giving.

"Church Difference Makers also guided our work with our bishop, Ruben Saenz Jr. Our consultant's understanding of the United Methodist structure led us to a healthy engagement with the conference during this important season of discerning the next pastor for Lovers Lane.

"We are thrilled that Bishop Saenz appointed Eddie Rester and extremely grateful for allowing our succession team to participate in the process. I believe our participation laid the groundwork for a successful transition and a jump start to Eddie's tenure as our new senior pastor."

These are achievable outcomes. But they require intentionality. The remainder of this book details how to achieve this success as a culture of pastoral transitions is implemented.

What Transitions "Not Done Well" Feel Like

Pastoral transitions not done well often start out fine because of the adrenaline in the church and among the exiting and arriving pastors. Sadly, the momentum fades away and situations arise that hadn't been planned for, ending in sad regret. Some years ago, I conducted a wedding that demonstrates this point. Our church had a beautiful outdoor amphitheater where the bridal party and all two hundred guests assembled following the ceremony. Each of us had been given a small flat box with instructions to not open it until directed to. Then, at the highlight moment, we all together opened our boxes.

To our surprise, each box held a live butterfly! When our boxes opened, the butterflies escaped, fluttering upward. Amazingly, as they drifted skyward, they bunched together creating a spiraling trail upward. We watched in awe. The butterflies symbolized the soaring aspirations, hopes, and dreams of the bridal couple and you could hear an audible "Ahhhhhhhhhh."

Until the butterflies cleared the top of the amphitheater, where they caught the attention of the thousand or so grackles nesting in the nearby Bradford pear trees. With a gushing swoop, the birds descended on the monarch butterflies now directly overhead. In an instant the "ahhhhhhh's" of their blissful symbolism turned into "uugghhhhhhh's" of things gone tragically wrong.

We know how fast "ahhhhhhhh's" can turn into "uugghhhhhh's." It happens way too often in a pastoral transition, when reality can devour so many hopes, dreams, and possibilities. The new pastor, the church, district superintendents, and bishops—the whole conference is looking at the possibilities and the future and the hopes and dreams of a transition when it gets started. The universal prayer is that it be done in a positive, productive way that results in church health and growth. Everyone gushes together at the start, "Ahhhhhhhhhhhh!"

But how quickly the "ahhhhhhhhh's" can turn to "uuugghhhhhhh's" when the handoff is poorly managed; when the church clings to the exiting pastor instead of embracing the newly appointed one, when the exiting pastor clings to authority and continues to insert themself into the pastoral ministry of the church, when the new pastor arrives unprepared to lead, when the newly appointed pastor is a poor fit and conflict emerges within months.

That's why congregations saying goodbye and hello must be trained and intentional. That's why exiting pastors must be committed to the church's future beyond their tenure and be diligent in understanding that clergy run a relay race, not a marathon. That's why arriving pastors must learn the culture and history of the church they are inheriting. That's why sensitive and well-trained cabinets must play a critical role in every pastoral transition. That's why a coach can be so crucial in navigating the process, because hidden realities can turn "ahhhhhh's" into "uugghhhhhhs" in a transition not done well.

Every transition is a bridge to the church's future. However, not all bridges are alike. Engineers identify six basic types of bridges—suspension, truss, arch, cable-stayed, tied-arch, and cantilever—and the type of bridge to be built depends upon unique characteristics of the gap to be spanned. So the type of bridge to be built will take advantage of strengths while leveraging the reality of existing conditions. No particular type is inherently superior; what matters is matching the design to the need and the challenges to be overcome.

The same can be said of a pastoral transition: a pastoral transition succeeds when the approach matches the church's particular needs and complexity.

Three Channels of Transition

Healthy transitions exhibit common characteristics: They are planned, agreed upon, and carried out with prayerful intentionality at every level. There are three primary channels through which pastoral leadership changes occur within The UMC:

1. **The Traditional Appointment Process:** The bishop, in consultation with the cabinet and SPRC, discerns and appoints a new pastor, usually from within the conference.
2. **Planned Succession:** With the bishop's blessing, a church promotes an associate pastor or engages in a broader search, sometimes beyond the conference.
3. **Succession Planning:** The local church intentionally prepares for leadership change in conjunction with the bishop and cabinet, mitigating anxiety and planting seeds for growth. This planning can (and should) accompany every channel of transition.

The first channel, the traditional appointment process, remains the most common and historically effective. But the other two represent growing opportunities that demand serious attention to achieve healthier transitions and stronger churches for many congregations in the changing church landscape. In the words of longtime church thought leader speaking of improving pastoral transitions, Gil Rendle, this process occurs "especially among our large and very large congregations."

The Evolving History of Appointment Making

Since the beginning of The UMC the process of deploying pastors has changed dramatically (see Charles Ferguson's 1971 monumental *Organizing to Beat the Devil: Methodists and the Making of America*). Dating back to the days of John Wesley, itinerant circuit riders were prayerfully assigned (appointed) by Mr. Wesley himself, and then later by an area's presiding bishop to an emerging mission field to pastor growing populations and plant new churches.

But there have been constant tweaks over the years and there is no reason to think those tweaks will or should end. Consider this seismic shift a generation ago: There are still older retired pastors who can remember the days when they only learned where they would be serving in the coming year at the "reading of the appointments" to close the session of the annual conference. Then pastors would scramble to move their family to a new locale, and churches would scramble to get the parsonage cleaned up after the current occupant vacated.

Dr. Lovett Weems humorously shared with me his memory of getting his first student appointment and learning where he was being sent at the closing session of annual conference on a Sunday . . . and having to start at the new church on Thursday! That short-notice approach to pastoral appointments lasted decades and was no doubt a spiritual endeavor but it also created enough chaos that improvements were regularly demanded and initiated.

Gradually, leaders recognized that earlier engagement with local church leadership was beneficial before a church received its "new appointment." As the world continued to change, Methodism became more attuned to the logistical need for a longer window between an appointment being made to when that appointment officially started. And that window would make for happier clergy families as well as local congregations. That window continued to widen and expand as consultations with the SPRC began to take more into account the rapidly changing world of women in the workplace and the embrace of female clergy.

Gradually, it became evident to denominational leaders that succession planning regarding a pastoral transition needed to account for school schedules of children and occupational realities of clergy spouses. Consequently, the once-revered "appointment reading" at annual conference morphed into "appointments season," which has continued to evolve to the point that many appointments are now made throughout the year for any number of reasons, including such realities as an unhappy match hampering the appointment, or unexpected events blindsiding the appointment.

As time went on, the consultation step of an appointment became a key role for superintendents who began the yearly "appointment season" with a thorough inventory of churches within their respective districts. Various tracking systems of "move," "stay," or "either" were developed to ensure the bishop and cabinet could successfully make appointments. Each district superintendent then would report to the bishop and the cabinet the results of respective consultations and the cabinet (the group of pastors serving as superintendents over churches within a defined geographic area) would work out together the respective appointments to be made with the bishop's guidance, input, and blessing. A successful appointment season in many conferences meant that the number of church openings matched the number of clergy available. And hopefully the pastoral match with a church would be considered a fruitful one!

The preceding short history demonstrates that the ebb and flow of making appointments has undergone constant change. In that spirit, we believe the time has come to change the culture of appointment making today to allow for emerging models of congregational participation in cases where church complexity calls for it. Culture can best be defined as "the way most people do most things most of the time." Our hope is to present such a compelling argument that ultimately most churches, most conferences, most bishops, and most pastors will become more intentional in pastoral transitions of all kinds.

A guiding principle of The UMC and other Wesleyan churches is that only the bishop can make an appointment. Regardless of the approach that hopes to match the right pastor with the right church, this principle remains constant. We champion this essential principle in our work—both preparing a church for transition, and when requested, conducting a pastoral search for a local church in partnership with the resident bishop.

In its current iteration in most conferences, the bishop and the cabinet, in consultation with the SPRC, does its due diligence and discerns (a) when the time is right for a change of pastors, (b) what factors should influence the selection of a new pastor, and (c) the timeline for "fixing" an appointment and subsequently announcing it publicly. In this way the appointment of each pastor to the respective churches is made with the prayerful hope it truly matches the right pastor with the right church at the right time for the right reasons.

Succession Planning

The term "succession planning" has risen in importance and frequency in almost every segment of American professional life in recent decades. It means advance planning for leadership change—ensuring that an exiting leader effectively passes the baton to a successor. Thousands of studies and papers have examined its practice across industries. In sports, in industry, in politics, in legal and professional circles, succession planning is a staple in the lexicon. The concept is universal even if its nuances vary by field.

In the church world, expectations of succession planning speak the language of laity who are professionals in their respective fields while being involved in local church leadership. It does not frighten them; rather it connects with their real-world experience. The following pages explain in detail the emerging and growing emphasis on (a) succession planning as a key concept for the church going into a pastoral transition. Initiating succession planning also promotes the practices of one of its key components, (b) "transition preparation" as a priority in The UMC's appointment system, and which every church could and should successfully do with intentionality, excitement, and effectiveness.

While succession planning, and—as we will learn—"planned successions" may not affect all churches, "transition preparation" is a *must* for every church during a transition. Succession planning and planned successions have both been around awhile and have plenty of examples, good and bad, from which we can learn. The lessons learned and the experience earned can help today's bishops, cabinets, pastors, and churches discern when, where, why, and how to implement these approaches with more intentionality.

These newer paths—encapsulated in planned successions and succession planning—are emerging options for appointment making, which are simply newer iterations of accomplishing the same goal as the traditional appointment processes: a God-honoring effective church led by a well-matched lead pastor to make disciples of Jesus Christ for the transformation of the world.

The Methodist movement no longer deploys circuit riders on horseback, even though we hold that era dear; we do not expect clergy to wait until the last day of the annual conference to learn where they will be serving and living within just a few weeks. So there is high value in embracing the slow, steady progression of how we go about securing the right pastor for the right church. This takes nothing away from the time-honored role of the bishop in making appointments; it just adds options of approach for the bishop in light of the changing church environment of today.

The environment is challenging. It is accepted that we must reinvent many denominational practices in our never-ending commitment to remain relevant and influential in both a post-Covid and post-disaffiliation reality. The resulting dynamic manifests itself today in conferences merging and reshaping in ways that take in more geography while simultaneously responding to budgetary challenges that often include reducing the number of districts and district superintendents. How realistic is it to assume we can be as effective as we once were in making appointments in the same way we made them before these major culture shifts?

Facing a shrinking margin of error in a more secularized world in which church participation is declining nationally, cabinets not only spend countless hours making sure they successfully make appointments, but they must also invest deeply to make those appointments successful. That's where succession preparation comes in as an intentional top priority as United Methodism claims a new viable future.

Planned Successions

In this book we are making the case for being more open to and intentional about planned successions becoming a mainline part of our appointment culture. Grounded in work with dozens of transitioning churches, our approach draws from a comprehensive report by Gil Rendle, presented to the Council of Bishops in 2010, titled "Clergy Transitions in Large and Very Large Congregations."

We have adopted his wisdom and findings, but our process is more than theory; over the past decade we have applied it in hundreds of pastoral transitions across the country, and more than a dozen senior pastor searches for larger churches.

Planned succession is different from succession planning, but the latter always springs from the former. Planned succession is often associated with moving up a highly effective associate into the role of senior pastor as the successor to a long-tenured, beloved pastor. Such was the approach in 2023 when Olu Brown, founding pastor of Impact Church in Atlanta, announced his retirement and urged his bishop to appoint one of his associates, Paul Thibodeaux, to become his successor. Not every church is right for moving

To explore Gil Rendle's full report, scan the QR code or visit the companion website at the back of this book.

up an associate into the lead pastor role or for a pastoral search. Actually, most won't initiate such a search. While every church would benefit from a succession-planning process—like our Changeover Zone—to see enhanced success, relatively few would be suitable for a pastoral search process under the umbrella of the planned-succession approach. Our typical appointment system has long proved its value in most cases. However, in some cases there are a few churches every year going through a pastoral transition that for a variety of reasons are more suitable for the planned-succession approach.

It is not because those few have more value than other churches, it's just that they noticeably have more complex systems. In such a complex system there may well be advantages to using a wider search process than what the typical appointment system typically uses. We recognize this truth and recognize that if there is not some kind of shared common system to meet the leadership needs of larger churches, then misunderstandings and resentment can emerge. It is likely that the church with the biggest budget and most perceived influence and power, which is seen as being "better than the rest of us" and operates on a different appointment system, will allow for resentment and divisiveness within a conference.

If larger churches are perceived as being free to go in and poach whatever pastors they want, that behavior will certainly create distrust and resentment within our denomination. We want to remove any stigma of "big churches" raiding or poaching, but we do want to create a system that satisfies the leadership needs of our larger congregations. Even The United Methodist Church of the Resurrection (COR), the denomination's largest church, sees the wisdom of staying within the parameters and protocols of The UMC. When they first engaged our services regarding conversations on succession planning, to prepare for Adam Hamilton's inevitable retirement, our earliest function was to hold a virtual meeting with Bishop David M. Wilson and the church's succession team. They emphasized not going around the bishop but working within the bishop's protocols.

More specifically, this book highlights a case study of Lovers Lane UMC in Dallas, which went through a highly successful planned succession in 2024. Their recent transition will be detailed in this book by their retiring pastor, Dr. Stan Copeland, and will include input from Stan's successor, Dr. Eddie Rester, along with key leaders who served on the succession team. Their observations will add clarity and reality to the principles, practices, tools, and techniques that I (Jim Ozier) will be sharing.

This detailed and comprehensive case study of Lovers Lane UMC covers 2023–2025, as the congregation strategically developed a planned succession upon announcing the retirement of long-tenured and well-loved pastor Stan Copeland. The search began in November 2024 and Bishop Saenz announced an appointment in late January 2025. You will learn the nuts and bolts of how we—the church, the pastors, the bishop, the cabinet, and the consultant—did it. You will hear extensively from Stan Copeland himself, as well as firsthand accounts from key laity, staff, and newly appointed pastor, the Reverend Doctor Eddie Rester.

The case for planned successions revolves around this truth: Eddie Rester feels just as appointed as any other pastor. But no more so! Even though he came to the bishop's attention by way of a nationwide search implemented by a local church's Staff-Pastor Relations Committee and leadership team doing their work closely coordinated with their bishop, and conducted by a hired search consultant, it conveys no special aura over any other appointment. Lovers Lane feels blessed to have him appointed, and the Horizons Texas Conference will be strengthened by adding a new pastor with his experience, character, competencies, and track record. He is just as appointed as if he had come from a neighboring church within the conference via the cabinet in consultation with the church's SPRC chair.

It isn't as though the sacrosanct biblically based sense of being sent and of being appointed to a particular church and mission field is changing. Rather, the way to get to that appointment is changing in some instances, responding to the changing church environment.

The changing environment of appointment making is complicated by expanding geography and the shrinking of cabinets. Judicatory and local church leadership realize it is not simply about who should be appointed to which church but also what process to use in making appointments as effectively as possible.

We are sharing the Lovers Lane story and our learnings with you because we believe this way of making appointments is an important contribution toward making a good fit between pastor and church. Planned succession represents another tool at the bishops' disposal. An added benefit is that the church leadership's impression of the bishop and our appointment process when engaged in such an intentional approach to an appointment becomes incredibly positive and exemplifies trust building. In addition, the laity involved in the process bear a deep commitment to making sure the new pastor will be successful

It's always been the case that there are occasional smatterings of planned successions that will happen outside of the norm of typical appointments or processes due to specific needs and unique situations. Many of these successions too easily create resentment and morale-crushing pushback among fellow clergy within an annual conference. This reason alone is why we are committed to building into our United Methodist appointive system a time-tested process such as the methods and procedures carried out by Church Difference Makers—a process that is replicable, understandable, and reflects the highest values of our Wesleyan heritage. It is a system that honors the bishop and the cabinet, respects all clergy and every church, and is in keeping with the long history of the Wesleyan tradition making a difference in the world!

As the country developed, Methodism moved beyond the circuit rider approach while clinging to its theological value of itineracy and pastors committed to "go where they are sent by their bishop." As the denomination grew in participation and structures, conferences approached the deployment of pastors with slight variations but always within the General Conference–approved protocols. We are fully invested in the same love and respect of our heritage, and we trumpet it constantly when working with a church. At the same time, we recognize that our future depends on openness to making the same kind of appropriate adjustments as our history reflects, to leverage our time-tested origins to meet the demands of our changing world today.

Transition Preparation

One of the healthiest enhancements being used increasingly and fine-tuned to meet the needs of a given conference's appointment making is "transition preparation." The UMC appointment process has always assumed that good preparation is part of a pastoral transition, but in recent years there has been more intentionality to this part of the process. This imperative falls within the broader term of succession planning, and denotes how the (a) local church, (b) exiting and arriving pastors, and (c) the cabinet work in concert and go about making plans and preparations for the transition from one pastor to another. Its effectiveness is found in including and preparing the entire congregation to understand and accept its role in a pastoral transition. Versions of transition preparation that focus mostly on the role of the exiting and the arriving pastors typically have more limited results.

Succession preparation grew in popularity with the late bishop John Coyner's *Making a Good Move*, Lovett Weems's *The Right Start* materials with the Lewis Center for Leadership, as well as our own work in *The Changeover Zone*. Many conferences now do their own annual version of preparation for pastors and churches involved in a pastoral transition. Still, way too many churches try to navigate the nuances and landmines of a pastoral change with a random, hit-or-miss approach. We hope to change that mindset with this book.

As we have mentioned, bishops and cabinets work tirelessly during appointment season to successfully make appointments. That appointment-making work begins with the hope that the number of churches needing a new pastor matches the number of pastors available for appointment. It is not easy to create and maintain a system where the number of new pastors admitted into the conference approximates the number of retirements; where the number of churches closed for various reasons is greater than or equal to the number of new churches started; and where the number of clergy positions available (e.g., lead pastors, associate pastors, conference staff) meets the needs of the conference context without becoming imbalanced. Beyond simply meeting the needs of pastors and churches, cabinets work toward successful appointments whereby every church receives a pastor or pastors who hopefully matches the church's culture, needs, and opportunities.

While cabinets always work toward healthy and meaningful appointments, succession planning and preparation help make the appointments successful! Unfortunately, most cabinet members are stretched so thin that they simply do not have the time to do as much as they would like when it comes to preparing their churches to say goodbye and say hello in highly productive ways. We have done succession planning through our "Changeovers Zone Training" for hundreds of churches and we hope our experience will become an important tool for superintendents to call upon when it comes to making their appointment successful.

When asked to do an autopsy of a pastoral transition not done well, our experience is that neither the incoming pastor nor the church has been adequately prepared—especially when the church is saying goodbye to a beloved, long-tenured pastor. Even in churches where regular pastoral transitions every three years or so is seen as the norm, faithful and engaged laity can be quietly dealing with burnout. Too often there is an anxiety-ridden skepticism in congregations with respect to what they sometimes perceive as leadership's assumption at play in congregations that any pastor can serve any church. Experience has taught too many laity in our churches to skeptically refer to this dynamic as "plug and play."

The lack of preparation leads to unforced errors that could have been easily avoided. Such errors elevate the congregation's anxiety level and can frequently lead to good members leaving the church—and maybe not just their local church, but leaving United Methodism, and worse, leaving church altogether. The stakes are sky-high to be intentional about succession preparation and succession planning. We will share some new perspectives on pastoral transitions that reflect succession planning and planned succession in the United Methodist spirit. The Church Difference Makers process is not some kind of change fantasy; this process is tried and true and while still new to many in United Methodism, we are confident this process will gain wider acceptance, just as the processes of using intentional interims has in recent decades.

Intentional Interims

The advent and wide acceptance of the intentional interim movement within United Methodism offers yet another example of the changing nature of appointment making. For the last fifteen to twenty years a healthy part of a planned succession frequently incorporated an intentional interim for a designated period of time to serve as the pastor of a church. Before the last two decades this process was rarely seriously considered in The UMC, and even scorned. "That's something Presbyterians do, but not us" was a common refrain in the halls of conference offices around the country as the intentional interim movement began to be openly discussed.

Today the intentional interim approach is applauded and widely utilized. Throughout the country there is a sophisticated network of training approaches and requirements for anyone considering becoming an intentional interim within a conference. Cabinet members rely heavily on these well-qualified and trained pastors (usually retired) who can serve part- or full-time for a few months or even years in particular church settings. The purpose is to serve as a bridge between the current pastor's exit and the next appointed pastor's arrival.

The placement of an interim allows time for the bishop and cabinet to work with the church to find the right pastor for full-time appointment; it may enable a church to grieve the sad loss of its pastor, or to heal from divisive conflict. The point is, the emergence of intentional interim ministry was an unexpected change initially met with some skepticism and resistance, but it has now proven itself to be a valued change in a changing world.

By their very nature, intentional interims often play a crucial role in a succession plan because they serve a game-changing role in the timeline planning for the church's next appointment. We believe that planned successions—when done with intentionality, training, preparation, and execution—allow for the same kind of impact as the intentional interim movement in a cabinet's appointment making.

Chapter 2

Guiding Principles and Empowering Tools

Jim Ozier

The changing church world is not just some benign shifting of ecclesiological practices and trends. Over the last two decades American church life studies consistently indicate that the era in which we are living cannot be glossed over as just a phase that will run its course and see the historic church right itself. Rather, all indications point to seismic shifts that portend ominous warnings for mainline denominations like The United Methodist Church. Statistics and patterns cannot be ignored or covered over with platitudes. The accelerating pace of change is pushing us toward a dangerous mix of uncertainty and irrelevance. Consider this October 3, 2025, headline from the nationally syndicated online news service, Axios: "15,000 Churches Could Close This Year Amid Religious Shifts."[1] Referencing sources such as Lifeway Research, the article points out that almost all of the churches closing are mainline, and the number of new churches launching is a drop in the bucket by comparison. No further disheartening data are needed here.

But we do need to remind ourselves that if The UMC is to remain relevant, one of the essential keys is to look with openness at our basic practices and ask: "Are there other techniques for accomplishing our historic values in ways that might be more relevant to the world in which we live?" Church leaders must explore updating systems, including how we approach pastoral transitions. That is this book's purpose: to motivate The UMC's leadership, pastors, and parishioners to improve our system of passing the baton from one pastor to the next; of building a bridge to the church's future.

The Francis Scott Key bridge in Maryland collapsed in 2024 after being struck by a runaway cargo ship. Officials called it a global crisis because of all the goods that travel in and out of the bay. The tragedy was about more than just one bridge; it intertwined with a wide system of connections and networks. Transitions function similarly, with a wide network of impact. It is seldom just about the "one thing" or the one church experiencing the transition, but about a whole series of interconnections—especially in a connected denominational system like The UMC.

No bishop would want to shepherd a system that approaches changing pastors in a church as a simple transaction to be undertaken randomly or without prayer and discernment. No local church leader would want an appointment change in their church to be perceived as a rote, by-the-book endeavor. Every bishop, pastor, and church leader whom we know wants their appointment process to be experienced as foundational to creating the kind of church culture that is relevant to people today in a changing world: professional, experiential, relational, relevant, and rewarding.

The following guiding principles are our North star pointing us to this culture creation for a church, and the accompanying tools derived from them can be applied to advance successful results.

Guiding Principles and Empowering Tools

We hold to five nonnegotiable principles that guide our work when helping a church navigate a pastoral transition, especially, but not exclusively, if the help includes conducting a pastoral search. Each principle is accompanied by a tried-and-tested tool available through the companion website that we use in our work with an SPRC or leadership team.

1. "Only the bishop makes an appointment": working with the bishop
2. "Not everyone, but each one": when to consider a pastoral search
3. "Respect all people in the process": working together
4. "Not the best candidate, but the right candidate": the Senior Pastor Focus Quadrant
5. "Trust is a must": cheerleading in the Changeover Zone

1. Only the bishop makes an appointment.

We make it a consistent practice to provide all churches with which we might work our written commitment to positively and proactively work alongside the resident bishop of the church undergoing a pastoral transition. The following information is provided to the SPRC and always championed by us among all stakeholders in a pastoral search:

- We do not work around the bishop or under the table; we only work with the blessing of the bishop and cooperatively with the cabinet.
- We understand we are working in a bishop's area and under the bishop's purview so the bishop sets the protocols for conducting a pastoral search.
- We require an SPRC to work in strictest confidentiality, while demonstrating complete transparency with the bishop.

To read the full "Working with the Bishop" resource, scan the QR code or visit the companion website at the back of this book.

2. Not everyone, but each one.

Not every church will involve itself in a planned succession process, but each church that does deserves a systematic approach that is well known and respected within the denomination. Each church that does need a pastoral search, because of its complexity and context, deserves to have a planned succession process considered—within the context of the "working with the bishop" section above. Any consideration of whether a church is given permission by the bishop to do a pastoral search should be done well in advance and follow these steps:

1. Either the current senior pastor or the SPRC chair, or both, should request conversations with the resident bishop and their district superintendent.
2. The conversations should be exploratory in nature.
3. One should be prepared to make a case to the bishop, rather than to make a demand of the bishop or expect any particular response.
4. Bishops have many reasons to agree to a search and many reasons not to allow a search to happen—honor the bishop's considerations and decisions.

Here are the most common characteristics of the churches for which it would be appropriate and for which it would be beneficial to conduct a search:

- A successor will be following a long-tenured beloved pastor, and congregational leaders voice outsized anxiety and concerns about the potential negative impact of a pastoral transition.
- The church's culture and its ministry focus are unique, well established, and closely identified with the current pastor. Leadership has thoughtfully wondered if the right successor can be found within the conference or through traditional means.

- There may be organizational or demographic cultural considerations that have stretched and stressed the church's systems, and therefore a transition poses an additional risk of major losses.

- The leadership team agrees that the church's nature and unique character might require a wider pool of prospects to consider than their home conference currently includes.

- The church's situation and setting may be perceived as fragile and in need of specific graces, gifts, experience, and talent not readily available within its conference.

3. Respect all people in the process.

A successful pastoral transition, starting with the search process, involves many stakeholders. Each stakeholder faces their own pressures and stresses that may be unknown to others. To be God-honoring is to always display empathy and compassion toward all the players—that compassion should be extended toward the bishop, the district superintendent, and their colleagues; the church staff; and the vast array of parishioners who may be lobbying for particular characteristics they hope to see in their new pastor.

A critical aspect of respecting all people among the SPRC or some designated succession/search team working under its auspices is confidentiality. Confidentiality is paramount and to embody its importance we suggest drawing up a covenant agreement on confidentiality that all members sign. As important as a "Working Together" agreement is, the greater value is simply to create a culture of respecting all people in the process.

To access the "Working Together" agreement tool, scan the QR code or visit the companion website at the back of this book.

And remember that respecting all people in the process means respecting all candidates who may be considered. Only one of them will come through the process successfully being presented to the bishop for possible appointment, so it is important to treat every prospect and candidate with honor and respect.

4. "Not the Best Candidate, but the Right Candidate."

Almost all the parishioners in a church are hoping and praying that their next leader is "the best pastor available." That is what they expect of the bishop and the bishop's cabinet as foundational to their appointment. The SPRC chair, the consultant, and the entire search process all expect to find the best available pastor.

However, one of our earliest duties as consultants is to help leadership understand that we see our role as finding "not the *best* candidate, but the *right* candidate." For churches of the size and complexity that are likely going to be given the okay to conduct a search, only outstanding clergy will ever be considered. Every prospective pastor lifted up for consideration is going to be a great pastor, a gifted communicator, an outstanding leader, and a likable person. This reality only makes the question that much more pressing: But which one will be the *right* one?

Of course, it is not our job as consultants to simply tell a church what is right for them. It is our task to help them discover and articulate what "right" looks like for themselves, so we developed a number of tools designed to help a team have healthy conversations to arrive at consensus on just that point. Our most basic is called "The Senior Pastor Focus Quadrant," which helps either the church's SPRC or search team, or both, tell us which ponds to fish in based on four loosely formulated categories:

To access the complete Senior Pastor Focus Quadrant tool, scan the QR code or visit the companion website at the back of this book.

1. steady pathway,
2. big break,
3. last hurrah, and
4. notable difference.

All of this is to help get some clarity on what the church feels is the right match for them.

5. Trust is a must.

When a church learns there will be a pastoral leadership change, that church enters the Changeover Zone, a period of time (ideally a hundred days before the new pastor arrives and for the first hundred days *after* the pastor arrives) in which intentional, thorough training is provided for (1) church leadership, (2) the exiting pastor, and (3) the arriving pastor. Throughout the entirety of the Changeover Zone, we are committed to strengthening a trusting relationship between the congregation, the bishop, and the cabinet. We are constant cheerleaders who emphasize that the bishop and the cabinet are valued team members in ensuring the best outcome for the church during a transition.

In most churches there already exists a healthy trust relationship, thanks to the diligence of a district superintendent's time investment with church leaders. We would be remiss, however, to not acknowledge that in many churches that trust relationship has eroded. We often hear leaders lament, "a string of bad appointments," or "they don't really care about us." In those cases the church culture has often turned negative or even toxic. In the midst of such a culture and comments we make it a priority to be a cheerleader for the future and to stress the importance of regaining and promoting trust.

Let's face it: With tightening conference budgets, we are seeing more geographic reconfigurations that leave bishops and cabinets with more responsibilities, and most district superintendents have more churches now than they would like—making it even more difficult to be in close connection to their local churches. The result can strain trust. So we stress the importance of intentionally rebuilding and strengthening trust, especially in the Changeover Zone.

"The Changeover Zone"—which is separate and distinct from a pastoral search—is a name derived from the track-and-field world, where runners pass the baton from one to another in a set of clearly defined lanes. In a track meet, "the Changeover Zone" is usually a distance—20 meters—where a series of well-practiced, intentional elements occur that lead to a successful passing of the baton.

The Changeover Zone for a church transition involves time: ideally one hundred days—but often less and occasionally more—in which a series of well-planned and practiced, intentional elements occur that lead to a great passing of the baton to a new pastor. Ignore the Changeover Zone at your own peril! Even in a transition where the church is given permission to conduct a pastoral search, the Changeover Zone preparation is often as important as the search itself. To think that a random, half-hearted, ill-prepared passing of the baton will not hurt the success of an appointment is just not realistic.

Our Changeover Zone workshop training is based on our book of the same title, *The Changeover Zone: Successful Pastoral Transitions*. Using the process discussed in detail there, we witness time and time again the level of anxiety decreased and the level of excitement increased. A church has few better opportunities to grow than when there is a pastoral change done well!

Managing the Changeover Zone is not merely about guaranteeing a smooth and seamless transition. Instead, we aim to create an environment in the congregation that leads to growth during the transition period itself. One way to focus on that growth potential is to think about a first-time visitor who happens to attend church during the Changeover Zone. Even if they don't know anything about the exiting pastor or about the arriving pastor or even about the transition, we want a process unfolding such that they walk away saying, "These are the kind of people I could hang out with." Someone making a relational connection with a congregation or someone in that congregation can move to greater involvement and sense of connection and choosing more involvement, often leading to membership. That's how churches grow today.

We often conduct Changeover Zone workshops on a conference-wide basis where all the clergy moving and all the SPRC chairs involved in a move participate. We also are often asked to work with just one church at a time. Usually, these one-on-one training sessions happen because:

- a beloved long-tenured pastor is retiring
- a founding pastor is leaving
- there exists significant problems within the church that express themselves as a lack of a trusting relationship with the cabinet and with one another, and substantial conflict often permeates church life.

Succession Planning and Preparation

In its most basic sense, succession planning can't happen effectively without succession preparation. They go hand in hand: planning and preparing for a change of pastors on the part of the congregation and the respective pastors. (Ideally, the district superintendent as well.) Part 4 of this book details this extensively.

In the last few years, succession planning has also come to refer to a church—with the blessing of the bishop—intentionally planning well in advance to move an outstanding associate up into the role of the lead pastor at some designated time. We have worked with many of these situations that can have great benefit because the associate pastor is already known and loved and steeped in the church's culture. A warning: while such a planned succession can have great advantages, there are areas where caution is advised in this role change and how it is perceived in the congregation. Hidden landmines can explode if you skip the critical step of involving an experienced third-party coach to assist with role and relationship clarity!

When succession planning is referenced to indicate a local church's possibility of passing the baton of leadership to a beloved associate, we are talking more appropriately about "planned succession," and it should be treated as such.

Planned Succession: A Two-Way Generational Experience

Succession planning and planned successions create generational impact. I can see an amazing example of this at the hanging birdfeeder in our backyard. The feeder consists of thin wire mesh formatted into a large tube divided into two sides; on one side the mesh is tighter than on the other side in order to accommodate different sizes of birdseed to satisfy different species of birds. The wire mesh keeps the seed in the tube while also allowing birds to peck and pull out the seeds. At the bottom of the tube is an aluminum bowl that both collects dropped seeds but also provides a rim platform upon which a bird can perch while foraging if it chooses not to cling to the mesh itself.

My wife and I watched in amazement at a several-months-long process. Two parent cardinals would come for the larger sunflower seeds in the wider mesh side; their beaks too big to get into the tighter knit side to eat the smaller variety of seeds. We watched as they built a nest and birthed three hatchlings that they dutifully fed for several weeks. Finally, their hatchlings grew brave enough to leave the nest. The younger cardinals with smaller beaks were able to go to the feeder where they could get seeds from both sides! That's when something amazing really happened: They would take smaller, tasty seeds and drop them to the concrete driveway under the feeder and then Mom and Dad would swoop down unencumbered and eat the new seed from the driveway. The parents who once fed the hatchlings were now being fed by their own young.

Feeding became a two-way, intergenerational experience! So it can be with a planned succession. An older lead pastor, viewing retirement on the horizon, can—with the permission and blessing of the bishop—plan to bring on (or sometimes promote from within) a younger pastor with the full intention of passing the baton within a year or two. The older pastor will feed and nourish the younger associate pastor not only in skill sets but also in the existing culture. And the younger pastor can feed and nourish the older pastor and the congregation with the kind of changes the church needs to remain relevant to future generations.

Sound idealistic? That is what happened at a church we worked with in Dallas. White Rock UMC's pastor of ten years, Rev. George Fisk, was within a year or two of retiring when—with the permission and blessing of the bishop—he brought in a younger (totally different style) pastor by the name of Mitchell Boone. Mitchell had been serving a smaller rural charge, and it was evident that he was skilled, talented, and had a pastor's heart. He came on as the associate—a new position funded by church members who intuitively knew that White Rock (once a prestigious church that had declined steadily over many years) had to change significantly to reach a new demographic.

It was immediately apparent to all involved in the process that Mitchell was totally unlike George. Mitchell brought both his energetic talent and his free-spirit culture. There was even some concern over how he would be received in this old-guard kind of church. But coming in as a young associate gave everyone time and space and the spirit of grace to get to know and accept Mitchell and he quickly endeared himself to the aging congregation.

George had been a beloved pastor for a long time; he mentored young Mitchell into the life and culture of the church. And Mitchell also mentored George in the challenges of the changing needs and new ministry possibilities. So one generation (George and the established congregants) fed a younger generation (Mitchell and big dreams and possibilities) who in turn fed them back. When George retired and Mitchell became the lead pastor, it was a seamless and successful passing of the baton. And the church thrived. Even when Mitchell initiated some out-of-the-box changes in both programming and culture, the church quickly bought in. So it can be in a planned succession!

Great Teamwork Is the Key

In a recent interview (*Morning Joe*, MSNBC, October 17, 2025) author John Levy highlighted the findings of extensive research detailed in his new book, *Team Intelligence: How Brilliant Leaders Unlock Collective Genius.*

After fifteen years of studying great leadership, he points out that in ccompany's research they found that "people relate more to the future they believe they can have, than they do to the present. The purpose of leadership is to motivate teams to work together to create the future they believe in."

At Church Difference Makers we love working with a church's leadership teams to develop a great pastoral transition. These teams believe that even while having a change of pastors, churches have great futures!

> To see "Typical Teams Needed in a Transition," scan the QR code or visit the companion website at the back of the book.

We have enjoyed great success in our approach, and none more so than Lovers Lane UMC in Dallas in 2024. In other sections of this book you will hear from the chair of the SPRC/Succession Team on how their team formed and worked together. But first, take a look at Lovers Lane's backstory leading up to their transition.

Chapter 3

The Case Study: Lovers Lane's Culture and History

Stan Copeland, Retired Senior Pastor, Lovers Lane UMC

On February 5, 2024, commissioner of Major League Baseball Rob Manfred announced his retirement from that lofty position . . . set for January 29, 2029! Five years in advance. Was he worried about being a lame duck? Or coasting? Or rumors? Not really. Instead, he realized a longer runway allows for all the necessary planning with MLB for identifying, preparing, and onboarding his successor. (Patrick Andres, in Sports Illustrated Feb 15, 2024)

Five years is not too early for the lead pastor of a large church to begin to seriously think about the impact of her or his retirement upon the church they serve. Five years is not yet a common time frame for planning a senior pastor transition; more often, the window is between two to three years, which is the transition timeframe Church Difference Makers recommended when it worked with St. Luke, a large church in Indianapolis. And sometimes it is even shorter – the Lovers Lane's time frame was only a year. As you saw in chapter 1, a key guiding principle is to determine when/if your church should even consider exploring a pastoral search for a transition. These considerations take into account the culture of the church, its past appointment history, and the complexity of its structure and ministries. The leadership team at Lovers Lane discerned it would be wise to speak with Bishop Saenz about getting his permission to proceed. Here's the story of why.

Appointment Reflections

Lovers Lane United Methodist Church (Lovers Lane), the congregation I (Stan) served as lead pastor for twenty-seven years and three months, has not always had the easiest transitions experience. Unfortunately, the last pastoral transition led to two years of negative press and all kinds of speculation.

So much for smooth successions. Such was the state of the church when I came to Lovers Lane. There were plenty of news articles out there pointing to conflict and challenges, leading many people to wonder if this flagship church was on a path of decline to no return.

I am the first to admit that when I was appointed to Lovers Lane at the age of thirty-eight, I never dreamed of being there for twenty-years and three months. Those last three months overlapped with my successor, the Reverend Dr. Eddie Rester.

> Check out the 1996 D Magazine article about Lovers Lane UMC and succession by scanning the QR code or visit the companion website at the back of this book.

Looking way back, two years into my first appointment as an associate pastor to First UMC in Henderson, Texas, as a very green twenty-six-year-old ordained deacon in the church, I was reappointed to First UMC in Houston. At that time First UMC Houston was the largest congregation in our connection, and I was appointed there largely to be close to MD Anderson Cancer Center, where I was being treated for what was then considered a terminal form of leukemia. I was ordained an elder, four months after my diagnosis and with a prognosis of three to five years left to live. It was a challenging, scary time, but you might only imagine what a miracle I considered it to be to stand in the marble pulpit of Lovers Lane United Methodist Church.

I began to think more intentionally about my retirement as I neared my twenty-fifth year as pastor of this remarkable urban congregation and into my fortieth year being an ordained United Methodist clergyman. At age thirty-eight, when I first arrived in Dallas, I never dreamed I would still be serving there when that time of retirement contemplation would come.

Longevity DNA

Longevity in pastoral leadership has defined Lovers Lane since its founding. Our first full-time pastor, Rev. Tom Shipp, was only twenty-seven when he arrived in 1945. The church had been planted a year earlier by a young student pastor from Arkansas, Rev. Bill Scroggins, and was meeting in a home with about thirty adults and as many children.

Tom, then an associate at Highland Park Methodist, had developed a passion for ministering to alcoholics. This was the 1940s when most church folk saw alcoholics as drunks who needed to get sober and clean up their act to be associated with "good people" in the church. When a group of Lovers Lane laymen sought funding from Highland Park for their first building, their pastor, Rev. Marshall Steele, agreed to help—but only if the fledgling church called a full-time pastor. He had someone in mind: his young associate, Tom Shipp.

The men appealing to Highland Park wrestled with the decision. They loved their student pastor but didn't know Tom. Legend has it they went to the Highland Park pharmacy, prayed, and drew straws. Tom was chosen. He arrived and soon his alcoholic friends followed, which sparked the church's first conflict. Some protested: "We won't be part of the First Alcoholic Church of Dallas!" To which Tom famously replied, "These people need us. If we're not here for people who need us, then why are we here?

And maybe I shouldn't be your pastor." The majority of the congregation sided with their young leader, and a culture of grace, inclusiveness, and courageous ministry was born.

A Unique Legacy

Under Tom's leadership, Lovers Lane grew rapidly. By 1968, the congregation was identified as the fourth largest in Methodism and was said to have at least 350 families of recovering alcoholics. Bishop Stowe observed Lovers Lane as one of the first predominantly white congregations in Dallas to welcome African Americans into membership—well before the Civil Rights Act was signed into law. Tom served thirty-one years until his sudden death at fifty-eight, just as the steel framework of the sanctuary—still the largest stained glass building in the United States—was rising from the ground.

The Reverend Doctor Don Benton succeeded Tom. Don often told me those first three years following Tom were the hardest of his ministry, but he stayed eighteen years in total. His retirement came earlier than he wished due to episcopal policy at the time that required frequent pastoral moves. He was followed by Rev. Dr. William Jennings Bryan III, a gifted and brilliant pastor, but one who admitted he was unprepared for the complexities of a large, multi-staff congregation. Bill's tenure lasted only two and a half years.

My Appointment

That's when Bishop Bill Oden called me. On April Fool's Day, 1998, I was appointed to Lovers Lane. Prior to that appointment, I was serving Pollard UMC in Tyler, where the church had grown, built new facilities, and launched two capital campaigns in my five years there. I wasn't looking to leave. Truth be told, I wasn't interested in Dallas.

But Bishop Oden was candid. Lovers Lane had lost nearly two thousand members in three years. Conflict lingered, and trust was broken.

He involved the SPRC deeply in the discernment process, even arranging for me to meet with dispirited members who had left the church. That transparency mattered, and it allowed my appointment to be received with hope by the congregation rather than suspicion. But the church had been without a lead pastor since January 1, 1998, and there was no formal succession plan at all. On my own, I connected with the only two living former pastors in Don Benton and Bill Bryan, who are both now deceased. I had lots of questions, and they had information that was valuable, but I did have to find my own footing, as all do in new pastoral appointments.

Culture Change Happened

One of the first things that I initiated was a visioning process with a lay-led team called the Power of One Task Force. The assignment for this team was to come up with a short-term plan (three to five years) that the congregation would approve and pursue. This plan would determine the ministry focus in four or five distinct areas and answer the questions, Do we have the staff we need? Will our facility support the ministry? Do we have adequate funding?

The ministry plan had much to do with how to attract and keep young families in the congregation. We didn't have the staff we needed, and the team shared my view that it was time to rebuild. The facility was old and tired and had not been adequately addressed for many years. We did not have the funding in the budget for staffing, nor did we have the funding for capital improvements. The church heard the report of the Power of One Task Force at the fall charge conference in 1998, and an architectural firm was secured to design a new building that would support the ministry the Power of One Task Force described in their plan.

Within thirteen months of my arrival as pastor, we initiated a $13 million building mission that was long overdue. There were many critics who scoffed at our goal, given the fact that just two years prior the church had raised about $3 million in a campaign in the midst of a very rocky time. The perception was that Lovers Lane was not healthy enough, nor did it still have the financial strength to undergo such a large fundraising pursuit. Lovers Lane exceeded the goal by $1 million—attesting to the concept that vision mobilizes resources.

Before the building was complete, we had secured new staff in the children and youth areas and the church started to grow, especially with young families. The church finances were coming in line, and the budget targeted the ministry plan with adequate funding. The building of the new Christ Family Center and other improvements to the campus, as well as giving the North Texas Annual Conference $1 million for its Vision 2000 campaign, was proof that Lovers Lane was still a very vital congregation with a future.

Shortly after the building was completed a family gave a large sum of money, and with contributions from a few others, we initiated an extensive marketing campaign called wannaknowwhy.com. The church had within its membership the creative professionals to lead this website-driven (before websites were nearly what they would become) initiative, and we hired a marketing manager to get our message on billboards, in magazines, on radio, and in television ads.

It was a stellar and innovative campaign where we featured photos of members and captions like: You Matter . . . Wanna Know Why? wannaknowwhy.com. Joy is Possible . . . Wanna Know Why? We featured the incredible story of the Weato family's journey from war-torn Liberia to Lovers Lane. We featured the story of a member who had struggled with addiction, another from the loved ones of special needs child, a mother who is deaf, a Desert Storm veteran, a gay couple and their daughters—all were families who found love and support within the Lovers Lane congregation. And in these stories, so many people saw themselves and started coming to Lovers Lane to find home.

Fast-forward twenty-seven years, and the congregation has a multicultural African fellowship, our 12-Step ministry became the largest classical recovery ministry in the world (nine hundred people recovering from addictions meeting weekly), a significant ministry for the deaf community was born, and LGBTQ people found a welcoming and safe space full of loving people. Lovers Lane became a congregation worshipping in seven weekly worship services on two campuses. Four more capital campaigns led to more new-facility enhancements, five high-impact nonprofit ministries, and an endowment that grew from $2 million to $25 million. This transformation made succession more complex—and more consequential—for such a richly diverse congregation.

Planning for a Healthy Transition

It was still easy for me to remember where the congregation was when I arrived on April Fool's Day, 1998. It quickly became clear that the pastoral transition from Don to Bill had been poorly handled. After looking back into their history, I realized that Lovers Lane had experienced only four lead pastor transitions in its then-eighty-year history, and all of them had been rocky with significant challenges. I resolved that when my time for retirement came, we would do succession differently—intentionally, prayerfully, and collaboratively with the bishop and district superintendent.

At the end of 2023, I met with Bishop Ruben Saenz and my district superintendent, Rev. Edlen Cowley, and asked permission to form what I called a "Pastors Transition Team." This team of trusted lay leaders would walk with me through discernment, help me plan what was next for me personally, and guide how the church could navigate a pastoral succession in the healthiest way possible. It would be a significant time with trusted friends to discern personally, and with great concern and care for the church I had served under six bishops by this time—Oden, Moncure, Norris, Bledsoe, McKee, and, now, Ruben Saenz Jr. Bishop Saenz agreed. And the Pastor's Transition Team was formed. It motivated me to "discern" . . . which is the precursor for a great transition. Over the next six months that team would give way to the SPRC creating a "succession team" to lead Lovers Lane forward, following Church Difference Makers' process outlined in part 2.

The Seven Sequential Steps of a Pastoral Transition

As we teach in our Transition Training workshops, any pastoral transition successfully builds a bridge to the church's future through seven sequential steps, even though the church or the cabinet may not articulate them or even be aware of them. We describe those seven steps as:

1. discerning,
2. decisions,
3. notifications,
4. announcements,
5. introductions,
6. in-boarding, and
7. onboarding.

For the complete Seven Steps resource, scan the QR code or visit the companion website at the back of this book.

During the same time that the incoming pastor is onboarding, the current pastor is "offboarding" simultaneously through steps 3–6. It is vital to follow the sequence of these steps! Ignoring them can derail a promising transition!

PART TWO

The Sequential Steps of Building a Transition Bridge

Chapter 4

Discernment

Jim Ozier

This chapter and those that follow will address the seven sequential steps of a transition. Regardless of the size or nature of the church receiving a new appointment, or how an appointment is to be made, the following sequential steps will take place. It is worth noting that many of the steps are happening at different levels by the church, by the pastors, and by the cabinet.

Discernment and the Pastor's Transition

Discernment precedes every pastoral transition, especially when retirement looms. Many transitions reflect a common scenario: a long-tenured, beloved pastor has arrived at the place of retirement. While that decision and its subsequent announcement may even be expected among leaders and many congregants, it can still be a time of grief and pain. For many, "their pastor" is the only pastor they've ever known, or the one with which they have connected the most—not only in the up-front role of the preacher and leader but also because of deeply personal pastoral interactions involving themselves and their families.

A pastoral transition is not a simple transaction in which the baton is passed from one leader to another. It is about building a bridge to the church's future through relationships woven throughout the entire church and its many intertwined family systems and organizational structures. Because of the unknowns, the uncertainties, and the stresses within the congregational life systems, it is not surprising that anxiety will probably erupt in both expected and unexpected places.

How the retiring pastor says goodbye either mitigates or magnifies that anxiety. When retirement is on the horizon, wise pastors focus on two key values: First, to discern and regularly message "My Next." Second, to discern and dedicate needed time and focus to address the key ministry needs that should be accomplished to prepare the church for a transition.

Saying goodbye sometimes takes weeks, or months within the Changeover Zone, for both the church and the exiting pastor. The longer the bridge, the stronger the support trusses must be. And the longer the tenure of the exiting pastor has been, the stronger the pastor's goodbye must be. I witnessed firsthand how Stan Copeland expressed this principle: At an important meeting during the transition, Stan stood before a hundred or so key leaders and said it plainly: "If you want me to do your funeral, you'd better die quick!" People roared in laughter, but they also got the message that when Stan said his final goodbye, he was leaving and wouldn't be interfering with his successor.

For a sample boundaries letter, scan the QR code or visit the companion website at the back of this book.

In a healthy approach, the exiting pastor communicates to the whole congregation a written "boundaries letter" so parishioners and longtime friends will not have to guess about what the exiting pastor will and will not do in the future. None of these goodbye principles should be cold and matter-of-fact but should come with intentionality—from the pastor's heart as she or he ponders the past, prays for the future, and discerns God's hand in their ministry. Every aspect of the process comes after intentional time for discernment on the part of the pastor, the church, and the bishop's cabinet.

Some bridges not only get you somewhere but they also take you somewhere, toward places of awe and wonder. I still remember walking across the famous "Mile High Bridge," a 228-foot swinging suspension bridge spanning an 80-foot chasm at Grandfather Mountain in North Carolina. It has been almost ten years, and I still remember it like it was yesterday! The incredible views and the majesty of the scenery move people to the kind of introspection and imagination that delves into the soul. It facilitates inward discernment about life and purpose and God's hand in it all.

The bridge of a pastoral transition can have the same impact on congregants. Make it memorable! Make it awe-inspiring! Build it so that people can look out at their community and context and see vistas of a future that brings their souls to life. This kind of bridge from a retiring, long-tenured pastor starts with discernment: when pastors look deep into their souls and look for their "Next," when church leaders allow God's awe and inspiration to guide them as they look for the church's "next," when bishops and cabinets breathe in the high altitude of hope and spiritual reflection for the church's next pastor.

That is why the pastor's "My Next" is the place for us to start. We provide coaching for the retiring pastor to articulate their "next" because it is so critical in setting a healthy culture for the church during a transition. Why? Because anxiety is bubbling up. It is natural that wherever congregants say to themselves: "I wonder how we go about getting a new pastor?" "I wonder if we will lose many people?" "I wonder when we will know?" "I wonder if they will be good for me, for my family, for the church?" Wondering can so easily lead to anxiety.

Pastors, you cannot control a lot of what people will wonder about, but you have big-time control over mitigating their anxiety in wondering about you: how you are doing, what you will be doing, what's in your head and heart. The reason for communicating your "next" isn't for information, it is for confirmation! Confirming that you—and the church—are going to be okay, regardless of the transition. There are two things people love going into an unknown future: confidence and confirmation.

There is almost a direct correlation: The sharper and clearer the retiring pastor communicated clearly about "My next," the better the environment of the transition. The reverse is equally true. In addition, sharing about your future invites people—members, guests, and even first-timers—to deeply engage with you. Sharing about your heart says "I trust you"; sharing about the ongoing evolution of your plans and dreams reinforces to congregants that your time with them has been more than a job, it has been a relationship.

That is why discernment is the beginning of any pastoral transition. Discernment is a biblical word, found more than seventy times in scripture. A discerning pastor may be soliciting opinions, but the process is much deeper. It includes researching, doing homework, praying, inviting in the Holy Spirit, giving due diligence, and leading to action. And remember that while the pastor is discerning, so also is the leadership of the church and the bishop and cabinet. All three entities will be discerning simultaneously. Discernment is essential before a transition even begins. Yet it is often overlooked or undervalued by many pastors and churches.

To access the complete BIG STEP tool, scan the QR code or visit the companion website at the back of this book.

Pastors, we provide the following tool to assist in your discerning:

As you will see, Lovers Lane and Stan Copeland were diligent in following the discernment process we lay out in our BIG STEP tool where we ask, "What is the current . . ."

- **Situation:** your own and the church's
- **Timing:** Is it the right time for you and your family?
- **Environment:** What is the general health of church, staff, and you?

- **Personality:** What is your unique, genuine style of saying goodbye?

While the pastor's discernment about retirement is essential, so is the church discerning about its life and ministry. So here's a quick glimpse of our BIG STEP tool for church discernment:

- **Setting:** the current reality of the church
- **Temperature:** the health of the staff and leadership
- **Energy:** the vitality and attitude of the congregation
- **People:** participation level attendance trends

To summarize, this chapter explains discernment's importance, identifies who discerns about what and why, shares discernment tips, and will now highlight how Stan Copeland and Lovers Lane went about discerning for their future.

The Case Study: Discernment for Lovers Lane and Stan Copeland

As a trained coach with Church Difference Makers, I (Stan Copeland) love to work with pastors during their discernment period because I learned personally the impact it makes. I have the joy of coaching retiring pastors like Rob Fuquay at St. Luke's and others on their "Next." Often, these outstanding pastors have been longtime friends of mine; we've shared a lifetime of ministry during some really good times and some very trying times. I coach them not because I am smarter than they are; I'm not. I coach them because an extra pair of eyes on their situation from someone who has successfully gone through the retirement process is a real benefit for them and their respective churches.

My discernment process included putting together a Pastor's Transition Team, about which I will say more later. I knew it was important for me to be clear about what I saw as the potential pitfalls of retirement at my age, with my energy, and my belief that I am not finished yet. All considerations of focus would first be about the future, "the Next," and not falling into the pits that would diminish living abundantly as I have always strived to do in Jesus's name. The pitfalls I considered included:

1. How is my identity tied up in my profession, and particularly my call as a pastor? I have been preaching since I was sixteen years old. I was ordained a deacon in 1983 and have been serving United Methodist churches under appointment continuously as an ordained pastor since 1984.
2. What happens when my authority and prestige wane or are no more, or at least operate very differently?
3. What will I do when issues arise that may require professional counseling to work through?
4. Is there enough money in my pension, investments, and assets to walk away from the security of a good salary and benefits?
5. What will my next steps be, both professionally and personally?

Meeting with this team of trusted friends and members of our church proved to be most helpful in making the farewell come into view and in making it as healthy and wholesome as possible. But it's hard.

Intentional Pathways

I (Stan) formed my Pastor's Transition Team with great intentionality. Some were chosen because of their official leadership roles on the church council, SPRC, or other significant positions they had faithfully filled through the years. Others were selected out of deep mutual respect and personal closeness. A few were invited because of their professional experience—law, counseling, education, and more. One member was a clergy colleague, not of Lovers Lane but deeply familiar with its culture, having gone into ordained ministry from within the congregation. I also sought balance—of gender and age, of long-tenured members and those newer to the church.

Together, this group became both my sounding board and my support. Some would later become part of the succession team, while others served only in this season. Each brought wisdom and perspective that shaped both my discernment and our larger succession planning. We met in homes. The agenda was mine to set, but the conversations were mutual. I spoke honestly about my excitement, my anxieties, and my questions. They pressed me to name what gave me joy and satisfaction in ministry and life. They knew of my love for farming, of the creative outlet I found as the "Picklin' Parson," and of my passion for addressing difficult issues—disaffiliation, societal injustices, and food insecurity. They knew my dream of continuing that ministry through a nonprofit I had founded with colleagues. They celebrated with me the blessings of family and my role as "Pop," and they affirmed the joy I found in traveling with my wife, Tammy, and in tending to her happiness. I shared openly, and they listened with genuine care.

Relationships Are Key

Relationships are at the heart of pastoral ministry. They are both the greatest gift and, at times, the greatest source of challenge and pain. As I looked toward my next, I knew that my discernment had to take place in the context of the past and with the people I had served so long. They would be my discernment team—the Pastor's Transition Team.

The transition team was clear that they were formed to help me navigate the important measures of retirement and hone in on the "why," while helping me avoid missteps and pitfalls. We began meeting in early 2024. Our meetings always started with prayer and ended that way. Our conversations were deep and meaningful, and along the way my transition team encouraged me to see a professional counselor. That step proved invaluable. Together, my counselor and transition team helped me prepare not only for retirement but laid the groundwork for the congregation's next chapter.

The intentionality of working with my transition team and focusing on discernment wasn't just a technique to utilize. It also freed me to dig deep into my soul. The result was writing a book from the heart. Here is one of the reflections in my book:

"There are those among us—strong in their quiet way—who need no title, no recognition, no place of honor. They are the salt of the earth, not to be seen, but who make the world taste right. Their labor is unassuming, their faith deep, and they have shaped the life of this congregation in ways unseen, but never unimportant. These are the folks who make a church not just a building, but a home. After twenty-seven years of serving alongside so many, one begins to wonder how to ever bear to say "good-bye" to so many good people, to those whose faces have woven themselves into the very fabric of your life.

There are those moments—the ones that come not by choice, but by the weight of the role you've taken on. As a pastor, you're called to be there, even when you don't know what to say, or when you don't know if anything can be said. I remember standing with grieving parents, holding the fragile body of a stillborn baby, and I baptized that child at their heartbroken request with a tenderness beyond me and beyond words. These moments don't fit neatly into the prayers or the rituals of the church. In that silence, in that sacred sorrow, what matters is not the rightness of the words but the depth of the love that flows, and the simple truth that Jesus was there weeping with us.

There are times of pure joy too, moments when a wedding is celebrated, when you hold the baby for baptism, and are in awe of the promise of the good things still to come. But there are other times, far more difficult, when the joy has been broken—when addiction, infidelity, or violence has shattered the bonds of marriage. These are places no one wants to go, yet as pastor, you go because you must. You go because the role calls you to be with them, even when you have no words to mend what is broken.

There are times when, with a parishioner's hand in yours, you pray the prayer of thanksgiving, knowing that the surgery has given life another chance. Then there are times when you sit with a young man whose body is being ravaged by cancer, and you realize that no prayer, no theological answer, can make sense of such suffering. You sit and you listen, knowing that there are no good words. There is only the quiet presence of God, and the shared space of grief that is larger than anything you can fix. The questions may come: Why does God let such things happen? And the answers, though written in seminary textbooks, seem hollow in the face of such hopelessness for a cure. In moments like these, the best you can do is to cry with them.

These are the moments—the sacred, the heart-wrenching, the joyful—that form a ministry that is not made of ideas or ideals but of lived experience. Saying good-bye is not just about the passage of time, but about the deep bonds formed through shared experiences and even in grief, there is knowledge that this parting is part of the journey.

I grieve not just the separation but for the love and life shared, which makes the good-bye feel permanent. As those called to itinerant ministry, we understand that leaving is part of our calling, even though it doesn't make it any easier. Grief, though painful, is also a gift; it shows us the depth of what we've given and received. Not being a Senior Pastor frees one from a lot of responsibilities, changes relationships, and emancipates to an exciting newness and "the next." —"Farewell: Tending to a Soul," *A Pastor's Reflection After 28 Years of Ministry Together and What's Next*

You may never write a book, but I highly recommend putting your reflections in writing. As Jim Ozier often says, "Don't get so busy finishing up your ministry that you miss your own retirement!" Let God speak to you about it and through it.

Shifting and Turning Plans

In 2019 the United Methodists had a much-anticipated General Conference to hear the bishops' proposal for going forward and beyond the decades-long conflict over homosexual treatment and involvement in our denomination. It was a catastrophe in my mind, as by choice I sat on the sidelines in St. Louis, not involving myself for the first time in years in the delegate-election process. I had also written a book with one of my associate pastors, Rev. Scott Gilliland, called Together, supporting the bishop's proposal for the "One Church Plan," which gave more local autonomy to congregations to choose how they would relate to members of the LGBTQ+ community in their contexts.

The conservative coalition won the day, defeated the bishops' plan, and put in place even harsher, more restrictive, and punitive measures that would ultimately lead to the splintering of the church. I vowed to do what I could to get involved in the 2020 General Conference, and I was elected to our delegation from North Texas. That General Conference was delayed for four very long years, and disaffiliation became the order of the day for The UMC.

I began to realize, as the years ticked down and COVID-19 ticked up, that this would be my final appointment. COVID-19 had a harsh impact on people everywhere and created patterns of coming together virtually, which transformed corporate worship and every aspect of congregational life. Even visitation in the hospitals for pastors became highly restricted. Funerals could not happen in person, meetings were conducted via Zoom, and people got accustomed to not coming to church, instead watching "the church show" in their homes. Lovers Lane was particularly good at creating online worship across our seven different services. Even so, giving became more of a challenge and managing budgets became a challenge even in post-pandemic life.

Professional Assistance

At one point, someone asked me, gently, "Do you think you might benefit from professional counseling?" It was a caring suggestion—and it resonated. Pastors are no strangers to moments when we feel ready to walk away. For me, the first such season came in 2006. I had taken a sabbatical to write a book about my mentor, Dr. William H. Hinson, who had died only three years into retirement. The book, *Lord, He Went . . .* (Abingdon Press, 2006), was nearly complete when trouble erupted back at the church.

A staff conflict led to the resignation of our music director and assistant. Though the bishop dismissed the charges filed against me as frivolous, some choir members departed angrily, leaving others confused. Then, within days, I lost a beloved associate pastor, Dr. Dudley Dancer, to Parkinson's. Soon after, a prominent family announced they were leaving, and I felt the weight of social status and gossip pressing in. For the first time, I was ready to cash in my ministry marbles.

I called Bishop Rhymes Moncure to tell him. Through my tears, I explained the resignations and the departure of this family. At the other end of the line, he laughed—loudly, uncontrollably. I was broken, and he was laughing. Then came the words that saved my ministry: "Stan, Stan, Stan . . . Lovers Lane ain't your church. Lovers Lane ain't theirs either. Lovers Lane is God's church. Now you get back down there and keep doing good work." Click.

That moment redirected my exit into a new entrance. Visits from trusted laypeople confirmed it. On their advice, I began seeing a psychiatrist. With her listening ear and careful treatment, I grew stronger and recommitted to pastoral ministry. That season taught me the gift of receiving professional help.

Through the years, I occasionally neglected to return to counseling, convincing myself I was "fine." But when my transition team raised the suggestion again, I knew the time was right. I found the perfect professional match to meet the moment: a psychiatrist familiar with our church, who loved the diversity and challenge of our Thrive service. Though she knew me better than I knew her, that connection became a blessing. I began seeing her monthly, and her guidance steadied me as I planned for retirement and discerned my next chapter.

I often joked with my transition team about reporting what I was learning from my "shrink." Humor helped disarm the stigma of psychological care. But behind the jokes was a pastor earnestly seeking clarity, courage, and health for one of life's biggest vocational shifts. Her professional insight, alongside the wisdom of my transition team, made all the difference in lightening the weight of retirement and opening me to embrace the next.

I took a renewal leave that summer, which included a trip with cousins to Scotland—a time of celebrating ancestry, prayer, and reflection. By September, after more discernment (and even a dove hunt or two with trusted friends), I had clarity about my future.

Chapter 5

Decisions

Stan Copeland and Lovers Lane Leadership

Discernment leads to decisions—and for me, to the decision to retire. It is vital that a pastor be clear about why the decision is made and what comes next. The more compelling and transparent that vision is, the more confident the congregation can be that the succession is healthy, Spirit-led, and ultimately beneficial not only for the church but also for our connectional United Methodist family.

I'm Not the Rocking Chair Type

I am too young—at heart and spirit—to retire from a life of meaning. Age may advance, but my resolve deepens. Retirement is not an end but a redirection. It is about leaning more deliberately into what gives joy, purpose, and contribution: standing for justice, advocating for the vulnerable, nurturing faith, and cherishing family.

For me, "the Next" will be guided by intention, not aimless wandering. Retirement is the chance to focus on the causes that have long stirred my heart, the people I love most, and the creative work that brings fulfillment.

Family First

Farewell to a congregation also means more time with family. Tammy, my companion of forty-four years, remains my anchor and my greatest delight. Together, we look forward to quiet mornings, shared travels, and simple joys. Our children and grandchildren are close by, and being "Pop" to Claire Marie, Lily Grace, and now Ellis James, is the richest calling of all. Lovers Lane has shaped their lives as surely as it has mine, and I look forward to investing in their faith and their futures.

Our home base will remain Dallas, but much of our time will be spent at Stillwater Farm—the one hundred–acre homeplace of my parents. That land has always called to me, and now it will be a center for family, ministry, and soul-tending.

Continuing the Work

I will always be a preacher. Though not in the weekly rhythm, preaching is part of who I am—woven into my soul. For five decades, I have stood before congregations more than four thousand times, telling stories, weaving gospel truth, and watching the Spirit move in silence, in laughter, and in tears. That calling does not retire.

I will continue writing—as I have since my first Upper Room contribution in 1993—books, cookbooks, and reflections. I will expand into podcasts and videos, with projects like Smokehouse Spirituality offering a conversational, homeplace setting for faith and story.

I will coach, mentor, and consult, particularly in pastoral succession and leadership with Jim Ozier and Church Difference Makers. The work inspires me, and I look forward to walking alongside pastors, churches, and bishops as they navigate change with courage and faithfulness.

Picklin' with Purpose

One of my deepest joys will be continuing to grow *Picklin' with Purpose.* Born during the pandemic, this ministry addresses food insecurity with dignity and creativity. From food clubs to Jammin' & Jellin' camps, from State Fair ribbons to partnerships with food banks, this work combines my love for faith, food, family, and justice. It is about others—preserving values that transform lives, teaching the art of canning, and making sure families have fresh, healthy food on their tables.

Homeplace and Sacred Spaces

Picklin' happens at my farm in East Texas, but it is not the only thing. Farming has been in the Copeland blood for generations, and it is deep within my soul as well. The farm will not simply be a retreat; it will be a sacred center. The Farmhouse Kitchen, The Porch, The Smokehouse, and the future Cookhouse will be spaces of hospitality, learning, music, and storytelling. They will echo my parents' lifelong invitation: *"Why don't y'all just spend the night?"* There, amid the smell of hickory smoke and the rhythm of East Texas soil, I will create, host, teach, and tend—to others and to my own soul.

Tending the Soul

Ultimately, retirement is about tending to the soul—guarding, guiding, and honoring the life God has given. My "next" will be about family, homeplace, writing, preaching, coaching, and outreach—about continuing the sacred work, but at a pace that allows for depth, joy, and reflection. This is not an ending, but a new beginning. Not slowing down, but settling into the fullness of who I have always been. My call remains: to live faithfully, to speak truth, to love well, and to tend both the souls of others and my own.

The Church's Decisions

I have shared some of my decisions springing from discernment. The church also had important decisions to make. First, they decided to go all in to accomplish the hard work of a pastoral succession. Second, they decided to do whatever it takes in terms of their personal involvement, time commitment, and teamwork to do what is best for the church. Third, they decided to set personal preferences aside and be fully invested in doing what is best for the church while being in partnership with and supportive of every protocol and decision the bishop ultimately made.

> See a sample Collaborative Agreement at the companion website included at the back of this book.

I continually drove home the truth, along with our consultant Jim Ozier, that no matter how hard the church worked in its search to always remember that the bishop may well know things about each candidate that we cannot know, so we honored the bishop's discernment and decisions.

The Collaborative Agreement formalized our bridge-building process and called for the formation of a succession team, and I saw my responsibility as naming that team. I consulted my executive pastor and executive director in selecting people to serve on that team. We would be committed to forming a succession team made up of SPRC members, the church council chairman and other leaders, members who had been here a long time and some who were fairly newcomers with a fresh perspective. Gender, race, cultural, and age diversity were valued.

Deciding on a Succession Team

The succession team assists the SPRC and works cooperatively with the bishop to build the bridge to Lovers Lane's future. To recruit them I first scheduled a call or in-person meeting, and spoke to each personally. Then I fol-

> To read the sample emails, scan the QR code or visit the companion website at the back of this book.

lowed up with an informative and affirming email to all who had said yes to being on the team.

Hearing from the Succession Team

The Succession Team members regularly updated the congregation about its progress. Here is an example:

Hello, I'm Jenny Anchondo Oakes, and a proud member of Lovers Lane United Methodist Church. I'm also truly honored to be part of our succession team charged with helping select our next senior pastor and say good-bye in the best possible way to our Pastor Stan and Tammy Copeland. My husband, Heath and I chose Lovers Lane as a place to raise our family. Brighton was on the way when we came and Gemma just arrived 10 months ago. Brighton loves Sunday School and Kids Sing and Gemma is getting such good care in our awesome nursery. Heath and I enjoy being a part of the Thrive worshipping community, and our friends we have made here. Enough about us. Let me tell you more about our Pastor Succession Team.

Our team is up and running. We had our initial full team meeting on the evening of November 11 from 6:00 to 8:00 and we got off to a great start. Our team is a diverse and talented group of 18 individuals representing a cross section of the entire church, and our 8 worship venues.

After spending some time getting to know one another, our consultant, Rev. Jim Ozier, introduced his company, Church Difference Makers, and the value they will bring to this important season in our church. Jim is a retired United Methodist pastor and in his fifty years of ministry served a large church in our conference and was on our North Texas Conference cabinet for seven years. He has dedicated his post-pastoral ministry to guiding churches through pastoral searches and transitions. He has wonderful relationships throughout the country that will serve us well in our process. Jim shared that he has already met with our bishop, Ruben Saenz Jr. and we have the bishop's full support in this process. Bishop Saenz requested that we try to complete our work by January so that we have proper time to plan and execute an excellent transition.

Jim then walked us through the key components of the process. We are currently in our preparation phase and have assigned subcommittees to help develop our church's "current reality" along with our prioritized "set of values" we hope to find in our next pastor. We are also leveraging the great work recently completed by our Power of One task force and Stan's last Pastor's Report to the Charge Conference to inform potential candidates of the vision and roadmap developed for our future.

Jim has also started what is called a "sonar search" to begin identifying potential candidates that might be a fit for our church. Jim's connections throughout the US are already yielding quite a bit of activity here. He reiterated what we all already knew that Lovers Lane is a wonderful church and one of the top recognized influencer churches in United Methodism. There is great interest in the Senior Pastor's position.

We got a lot of work done and know we have much work left to do. The entire team is prayerful and enthusiastic. We are committed to a thorough and transparent process. Please also understand some components of this process require a strict adherence to confidentiality, as one might expect in dealing pastoral changes. We will look forward to sharing regularly what we can share and know that we covet your prayers in our work and for our great congregation. You can go to the website llumc.org click the about tab and open the succession folder there you will find our posted material. Transparency is our value and you will hear directly from us concerning our process. Thanks for your time and interest.

As Jenny often proclaimed to the Lovers Lane congregation during this process, transparency should be of high value in any pastoral transition, while at the same time honoring appropriate confidentiality. Building a bridge to the church's future implies it is going somewhere and there is a strategy to get there.

Politicians often try to score political points scorning a "bridge to nowhere." A bridge to nowhere has one or both ends broken, incomplete, or unconnected to any destination. Making a bridge useful requires a definite, agreed-upon strategy. This reality is never more apparent than in building a pastoral transition bridge—yet it is often the most overlooked aspect of pastoral change. Where are we? Where do we want to go? How will we get there? The sequence of decisions to answer those questions not only displays a church's culture but also creates the strategy, which must be followed closely and communicated regularly.

Listening to the Staff

It is incumbent upon all parties building the bridge to not take communication with the staff for granted; the church staff is vital—and often feels overlooked—in transitions. Here is some of what the Reverend Kay Eck, Lovers Lane's outstanding executive pastor, shares about this dynamic in her heart-felt observations:

> To read Kay Eck's complete observations, scan the QR code or visit the companion website at the back of this book.

> For the congregation, Stan's retirement announcement was met with affection, gratitude, and the sadness that accompanies any goodbye to a long-tenured leader. For the staff, however, even though he shared his decision with the us just prior to the public announcement, this news opened a more complex emotional and organizational landscape.

Stan's announcement created a liminal space for the staff. The future was visible but not yet defined. People continued their work with dedication, but every hallway conversation carried an undercurrent of the unknown. Staff members wondered—not unreasonably—what the retirement of a senior pastor of nearly twenty-eight years would mean for them, their ministries, and the long-term identity of our church.

By November, we had taken an important step forward by bringing in Rev. Jim Ozier as our consultant. Jim's credibility, experience, and calm, practical wisdom were needed gifts for the process. Around the same time, the lay succession team was beginning to form. Their presence brought structure to a process that, until then, felt unknown.

Even with these pieces in place, the staff continued to wrestle with the emotional realities of transition.

They noticed that no staff—including myself—were included on the succession team. While this aligns with established best practices for pastoral transitions, it nevertheless elevated staff concerns.

They wondered whether their insights would have any space to inform the discernment of our next senior pastor.

Even though Jim and the chair of the succession team both held occasional all-staff update meetings, the anxiety persisted.

From the staff's perspective, our church was put on an accelerated timeline and this sped-up process raised genuine questions. Could the unique identity of Lovers Lane, shaped by years of ministry, be fully comprehended and protected?

These questions were not rooted in distrust of the bishop, the lay team, or the process. They were rooted in love for the church and a desire to ensure that the next leader would build upon the extraordinary legacy already in place.

Beneath all these concerns lay a deeper anxiety, though—one rarely spoken out loud, but almost universally felt: the fear of job insecurity. When a new lead pastor arrives, particularly after a long-tenured one, staff members know that organizational charts may shift. Priorities may change. A new leader may want to restructure, reassign, or bring in people they already know.

Staff understood this reality intellectually, but emotionally it sits much heavier. Questions emerged quietly: Will the new pastor understand the value of what I do? Will they want to keep me? Will everything I've built here continue?

These are human questions, born out of vulnerability, but also out of deep commitment. The staff at Lovers Lane love their ministries. They love this congregation. They have invested their hearts, energy, and lives in this special church. The thought of instability or loss during a period of transition—even if only imagined—was a real source of anxiety and fear for many on the team.

I also tried to create space for staff to voice their fears, either directly to me or in quieter moments of conversation. Even when answers were limited, being heard mattered.

The succession process that unfolded at Lovers Lane ultimately became a story of collaboration—of laity, clergy, staff, and denominational leadership working toward the same goal: a faithful handoff from one beloved pastor to the next, who has quickly become endeared to the Lovers Lane staff, I might add!

Eddie Rester has been welcomed enthusiastically and has done an incredible job; he is just what the church needed!

During a transition, we never want the church staff to feel like this bridge is going nowhere. Fortunately, that did not happen at Lovers Lane, thanks mainly to Kay's strong leadership echoed by the other executive staff members. My organization learns much from our debriefs with people like Kay, and this we learned powerfully: Even when the staff is ecstatic at the end result, a sense of "going nowhere" among staff can spread to other church leaders they influence and trickle into the congregation, doing great harm to the church's culture. So before decisions are settled and announcements made, take great care in the process as it unfolds, and communicate with and listen to all stakeholders, especially the staff.

Chapter 6

Notifications, Announcements, and Introductions

Jim Ozier

Announcements, notifications, and introductions are woven strategically throughout the transition process. While tightly interwoven, they must be separated to grasp their individual impact. The pattern expresses itself as follows: [Note that steps 1–3 have to do with a pastor's retirement; steps 4–6 have to do with the appointment of the successor.]

1. *Before* a transition begins, the senior pastor notifies the appropriate people about her or his retirement plans, including (a) the district superintendent (DS) and bishop; (b) the Board of Ministry; and (c) their SPRC chair.
2. Upon the bishop's approval, the senior pastor announces retirement plans publicly in appropriate venues for the church and the annual conference.

3. Either the DS or bishop, or both, will notify the SPRC chair of next steps and together they will design a communication plan for announcing next steps to leadership and the congregation.
4. *After* the church's new pastor has been duly determined by the bishop and cabinet (sometimes with agreed-upon input from a church's pastoral search), the bishop will notify the SPRC chair of their impending appointment.
5. The bishop will immediately establish a schedule of when either the SPRC chair or the DS, or both, may notify others in the church, and when and how the successor may be announced publicly. This schedule will take into account the need for the incoming pastor to notify their current congregation that they will be leaving. *This is a delicate step for courtesy and coordination purposes and must be followed carefully.*
6. Only after the successor has been duly identified and officially appointed may the church coordinate with their new pastor and the DS to initiate a plan of public introductions of their new pastor and family (if applicable.)

Throughout this process, the church must update the congregation positively while respecting necessary confidentialities. Within the above framework, here is a deeper dive into best practices when it comes to the when and how beloved, long-tenured pastors announce their retirement plans to the congregation:

Announcements

Rather than presenting a long-tenured pastor's departure announcement as a matter-of-fact event, it is far better to leverage this big decision into a marker moment in the life of the church and pastor, so it needs to be done with intentionality and care. Why? Because when and how a pastor goes about saying goodbye is a great way to reflect and strengthen the church's culture, while modeling healthy God-honoring relationships.

For the teaching tool on announcements, scan the QR code or visit the companion website at the back of this book.

The focus is on setting the when and how to announce upcoming retirement or departure plans, not just the date itself. Our experience shows that a pastor's goodbye should unfold as a series of intentional, strategic steps rather than a single event.

Announcement first in worship or social media?

Retiring pastors (and cabinets) often struggle with the basic question, Should retirement announcements be made (a) first in public worship and then followed up with email or (b) first by an all-church email followed up with more info in worship?

The remainder of this guideline speaks about this question in detail, and either way can work. But the best rule of thumb is generally to allow people to hear and process shocking or unexpected news in private, rather than in public.

It is often assumed that making the big announcement in worship first is more personal and lets everyone know at the same time. There are several problems with this approach:

1. That announcement will only reach those attending on that Sunday—typically a small percentage of the congregation. Plus, everyone in attendance hears the news through their own filters and shares it by word of mouth or social media . . . *with their own personal spin.* The result is that leadership loses control of the message.

2. It is more considerate to let people hear and process such news privately in writing or on video, then they can discuss it and process it in a family setting. Public announcements make natural responses harder—one person may grieve while the next celebrates or dismisses the news. First-time guests get caught in this emotional awkwardness and may be less likely to return.

3. An all-church email sent a day or two before Sunday lets the pastor and church control the message, ensures everyone hears simultaneously, and typically increases worship attendance the following Sunday.

Here is an excellent example of a retirement announcement and the reasoning behind it:

The best 6-Step strategic process will be something like:

Step #1: Pastor and leaders (including the bishop) decide on public announcement dates. The preceding days are carefully planned. This is a big deal!

Step #2: The pastor and family make personal calls to those especially close to them. Something like, "In the next day or two an email is going out announcing my retirement plans. I have not set a retirement date yet, but I wanted you to hear it from me personally. . . . Please keep this confidential to honor the process we want to follow to share this. Thank you."

Step #3: The pastor shares the decision with key leadership groups, timing the meeting a day or two after personal calls. This allows the pastor to share with key leaders something like this: "In the next day or two an email is going out to the entire congregation announcing my decision to retire in the coming year. An exact retirement date has not been set, but I wanted to share this news personally with those of you in leadership, before the email goes out. We want to be clear and strategic, so please don't jump the gun and start calling your friends! Allow the SPR's email to share the news with the congregation."

Step #4: The SPR/transition team sends an all-church email the following day, closing with something like, "Our pastor will share more in worship this Sunday." This typically ensures a full house! (See note in Step #6.)

Step #5: Pastor shares in worship the Sunday right after email goes out; some churches like to have the chair of the SPR or some other official also participate in the announcement. We recommend the pastor make a creative and compelling retirement video that is shown during the worship service and put on social media outlets. (Church Difference Makers website carries excellent examples from several churches.)

For an example transition timeline, scan the QR code or visit the companion website at the back of this book.

Step #6: Church immediately posts on website and social media pertinent information; the SPR/transition team's email was the matter-of-fact information concerning how the transition team will proceed over the coming months. Within a few days the pastor sends a personal follow-up email assuring the congregation of an orderly and intentional process. [Note: Some retiring pastors prefer to reverse the sequence so that the first church-wide communication come from the pastor; the second communication coming from the SPR/transition team. Either way is sufficient.]

Timing is key! Set the Sunday announcement date first, then work backward to plan each preceding step.

This strategic process addresses several critical dynamics:

1. For many in the church, the only senior pastor they have ever known is leaving. Create a safe, considerate atmosphere that reflects the church's thoughtful culture. Remember:
    a. Most people will grieve, and people grieve in their own way at their own time and pace.
    b. Many people will be flooded with memories, including pastoral moments in which the pastor performed their wedding, baptized their children, buried their loved onesand so on.
    c. Some may think, "It's about time"—even while loving the pastor. These mixed feelings need space to surface.
    d. A few people may put a bad spin on it. In any organization there are those prone to conspiracy theories: "So why is our pastor leaving *now*?" "So they finally forced the pastor out." "Hmm. Wonder what's going on?"

2. Don't forget first-time guests present the Sunday the pastor shares these intentions! This is why it is better for the sequence to be that people first receive and process impactful news in the privacy of their own home via email . . . then learn more about it publicly in worship. Some people will be in shock; some in disbelief; some expect it; some will be grieving; some angry. Who knows? This sequence allows members to process privately and personally in conversations (especially with children) as a family. The pastor will say something like this in worship: "We always have many first-time guests in worship and we are so pleased you are here this morning. You probably didn't receive the email that went out last week to our membership that I am announcing I will be retiring sometime in the coming year. Not to worry! We have a great leadership team that has already laid out a plan on finding and welcoming my successor in great ways! It will be an exciting time for our church."

3. Pastors often fear being seen as a lame duck after announcing departure, but experience shows the opposite: They are driven to leave a strong legacy and work intentionally with church leaders not only on that legacy but also to ensure a strong passing of the baton. Most long-tenured pastors are driven and hardworking by nature; that rarely changes because of an impending retirement.

    a. Announce sooner rather than later. First, retirement announcements allow the church to celebrate with the pastor for months before the final goodbye. During holy seasons, the pastor can share moments like "This is my last Christmas Eve with you wonderful people." Second, the clergy grapevine moves fast. Delayed announcements often result in haphazard disclosure through rumors rather than intentional planning, leading to awkward explanations and hurt feelings.

    b. Give the exiting pastor meaningful input into the succession process. While they cannot choose the successor, they have a vested interest in the outcome and deserve appropriate consultation with the bishop and church leadership.

4. Allow the pastor, especially when it is a retirement, the joy of personally sharing this deeply personal decision. A long-tenured retiring pastor and family are processing a major life transition.

   a. Even when a retiring pastor is ready to go and excited about entering a new chapter of life, he or she may experience their own unexpected waves of grief: the sadness of changing relationships; the uncertainty of what will happen to "the baby"; the loss of the pastoral role, prestige, and authority; the recurring pain of possibly wavering or second-guessing the retirement decision.

   b. The pastor, spouse, and children have formed deep relationships with parishioners through years of shared ministry and life. The pastor should have meaningful ways to share the news with these special connections, not just the bare information.

5. Give the laity a highly visible role in planning and executing the transition, reflecting the church's culture of honored lay leadership.

   a. When a long-tenured pastor leaves, it impacts the church as much as—if not more than—the pastor. Reinforce to members and guests that the church "is the people" and will continue moving forward. This is a key teaching moment. The laity's perspective must be honored in all things transition!

   b. Often, the key lay leaders are experienced professionals in leadership and transitions; this expertise provides insight where the pastor may have blind spots. Similarly, either the pastor or consultant, or both, can provide insight where laity have blind spots. Success requires partnership built on trust and respect.

   c. Significant transitions always bring some anxiety. The announcement period is a great time to forge and demonstrate that partnership between the clergy and laity.

   d. Successor selection succeeds when the process respects the congregation's state of mind, honors relationships, keeps everyone informed, and reflects intentional care.

6. The most important element in any pastoral transition is for leaders to maintain a consistently positive attitude! Never complain or criticize openly about any aspect of the transition.

   a. There is so much that we can't control: pandemics, denominational uncertainty, social unrest . . . and so much more. We control one thing: our attitude. This requires accountability.

How Stan Notified the Church

I announced my retirement via video posted by the church, knowing it would spread widely. It also allowed us to control the message. There was also electronic communication that was shared and easy for others to share. There are always some who need to hear the news directly from me and I make myself available for questions and comments from family and friends.

Although video and email controlled the initial message, rumors spread through Methodist networks as they always do. Rumors from other conference clergy swirled, saying that the succession process was all a sham and that one of the associate pastors had already been chosen as my successor. This was painful to many, misleading, and fabricated. So Stan chose to address it directly and pastorally.

> First, I want to thank you for the great work and tireless efforts you have put into the all-important work of succession. I want to say the team has my total confidence, and I will support your choices 100 percent. I have been very removed from the process by design, and Jim has kept me appropriately informed but not related to the confidential nature of your work. I did not know who would be the three candidates until I was told yesterday, and I have had the pleasure of visiting with each of them at their request and with the Succession Team's blessing. I only talked with one other prospect in the process at Jim's request. My visits have all been at their request and Jim's direction in lining up the calls. In all cases I answered questions to the best of my ability and had very positive interaction with each candidate and prospect.
>
> This coming week I would like to meet with each member of the team in groups of four or five for a breakfast or lunch meeting. My agenda is not to question or second guess you, but to hear from each of you about your perceptions regarding the candidates' strengths and the excitement about your choices. Here is why: I commit to be totally supportive of whoever the bishop ap-

> points based on your work. I look forward to publicly promoting the new pastor to the congregation, therefore I want to hear from you about them to be better informed and to reflect your excitement. Plus, I want you to be able to say at the appropriate time to all your friends and circle of influence how pleased I am with who the bishop appoints as my successor!
>
> Understand, it is not my place, nor is it my desire, to influence the choice, which will already have been made. I just want to be your choice's best cheerleader in the church and the conference! Again, I am comfortable with the three candidates you have chosen and by the time of the breakfast and lunch meetings I will know your rankings. Still, we all understand that Bishop Saenz has interviewed them also, and ultimately he makes the appointment. I believe that he also has confidence in your work. Please let me know which meeting you can attend, first choice and second choice please. [and then we listed meeting options]

Stan's goal was to champion his successor and intentionally cultivate unity throughout the church. This unity came not just from enthusiasm but from his active, positive participation in every step—except the search itself—to promote a remarkable transition. Remember: A church has very few better opportunities to grow than during a transition done well.

Make the transition memorable—a marker moment in the life of the church that celebrates unity of past, present, and future. This concept is evidenced by one of the most famous bridges in America: Michigan's Mackinac Bridge, built in 1957 to connect Michigan's Upper Peninsula with the rest of the state. It spans five miles over the water that connects Lake Michigan and Lake Huron, two of the Great Lakes. Its construction became a marker moment in Michigan's history and today millions of visitors each year come to drive over it, happily paying the toll. At its spectacular opening, speakers celebrated it as a symbol of unity.

A great pastoral transition does the same: it is a marker moment—memorable, inspiring, and reflecting the unity celebrated in scripture, "now they were all of one accord" (Acts 2:1 NIV). As you will see, introducing the new pastor must be done intentionally and strategically: one end of the transition bridge says goodbye; the other says hello.

Here is Stan's creative and compelling introduction of his successor:

SUNDAY, FEBRUARY 2, 2025

I'm excited to share that Bishop Ruben Saenz Jr. has appointed the Reverend Dr. Eddie Rester as the next senior pastor of Lovers Lane United Methodist Church! After careful consideration of several highly qualified candidates from across the nation, the bishop and his cabinet have chosen Eddie, who is one of the most respected and revered pastors in our denomination. Eddie is coming from the Mississippi Annual Conference. Welcome Eddie, and as we say, "A great day is coming soon."

Next week, Eddie, through a video, will introduce himself to us and also he will introduce his wonderful wife, Audra, and their two young adult daughters. I'd like to express my gratitude to the succession team for their thorough work throughout this process with our Bishop Saenz leading the way. I want to thank our consultant, Rev. Jim Ozier, who is preparing us for this important passing of the baton and training us for the Changeover Zone that we have now entered.

Yesterday, our district superintendent, Rev. Edlen Cowley, met with the Staff-Parish Relations Committee and the succession team to announce the bishop's appointment and introduce Eddie. Following that meeting, Rev. Cowley and Eddie met with our staff to share the exciting news of the appointment and give us time to hear from Eddie and ask him questions via Zoom. There were some great questions and a lot of enthusiasm about his appointment.

We'll all have the opportunity to see Eddie's video and get excited too next Sunday. I look forward to what's ahead for our church family! Please join me in daily prayer for Eddie and Audra, as they plan to move to Dallas and shepherd this great church—

you. Also, let's show our thanks and gratitude for the tireless work of our Bishop Saenz and DS Cowley in caring for Lovers Lane UMC in this all-important time of our senior pastoral transition. We simply could not have been led better. Thank you Bishop Saenz and Rev. Cowley. (Applause).

Chapter 7

In-boarding, On-boarding, and Off-boarding

In-boarding

For some time now The UMC has grown more intentional about on-boarding a church's new pastor, but only recently have we focused on the importance of in-boarding:

- In-boarding is the period between announcing the new pastor and their arrival to begin ministry.
- On-boarding occurs immediately following the start of the new pastor for a designated time to learn the history, culture, and current reality of the congregation.

Both carry great value. As our colleague Jim Griffith—whose track record in equipping new church starts is exceptional—says often in his workshops: "The church's new leader comes as their 'minister' and must earn the right to become their new 'pastor.'" In-boarding and on-boarding begin the process of that happening.

In-boarding's purpose is to help the congregation develop genuine affection for their new pastor before arrival. Why does this matter? Because many parishioners, right after they learn there will be a change of pastors, are making decisions about whether they will stay or go; about their future involvement; about their attitude toward and openness to receiving a new leader. The period between announcing a new pastor and their arrival is more fragile than most realize. In smaller communities, other churches of other denominations sometimes actively recruit your members during this time and in larger communities parishioners can be tempted to look around at other church possibilities during this time of uncertainty. In almost all settings, once the new pastor is announced, people are going online to learn more about them, and they can unwittingly develop a skeptical or cautious attitude. In-boarding can temper all the above possibilities.

A wise church invests significant intentional effort in in-boarding their new pastor, building positive anticipation before they even arrive. The most effective approach includes these practices:

- Show videos of the new pastor and family on worship screens—simple biographical content with the pastor expressing excitement. Their value grows when the current pastor gestures at the screen and says, "Aren't we fortunate to have ________ as our new leader?"
- Make videos of the current pastor with the successor; it is best to show funny videos that the exiting and arriving pastor do together. Be creative!
- Use selfies on the screens. When your successor makes a visit to see the church and facilities, be sure to take them around to important places in the community. Get a selfie of both of you together, a great way to bless your successor!
- Be sure to post the videos and selfies on all your social media accounts; photos can even be included in printed materials.

- Preach sermons about transition in the Bible and the value of a pastoral transition. Sprinkle in personal affirmations about your successor.

Be creative and enjoy the in-boarding process—but remember that the incoming pastor is still leading their current congregation. Limit meeting invitations thoughtfully.

In-boarding and onboarding merge effectively and create their own bridge to a seamless transition through the Listening Tour, which helps the new pastor learn the church's history, story, and culture. The Listening Tour is a way to enable the new pastor to meet with small groups in members' homes over a designated period of time. The Listening Tour is planned before the new pastor starts but conducted after they arrive.

A key part of in-boarding is publicizing the Listening Tour schedule and collecting sign-ups. This signals a consistent, intentional approach throughout the transition. Listening Tour sessions are arranged with the incoming pastor to ensure coordinated, well-planned scheduling. *The Listening Tour is detailed step-by-step in our book on The Changeover Zone.*

On-boarding

Every organization—corporate, nonprofit, or professional—recognizes how critical on-boarding a new leader is. What once used to be a random, "throw them into the deep end of the pool" approach to taking the reins of leadership has now become much more intentional. Its purpose is to familiarize the new leader with the culture, history, and practices of the organization. The best on-boarding processes—like that used by Claire Bowen, (now at the Candler Center for Christian Leadership) used in many conferences and with whom we occasionally partner—allow staff and key leaders to candidly address conflicts and unresolved issues.

On-boarding as an intentional process typically spans a few weeks to three months. In some cases, as in Lovers Lane, churches will elect to include an overlap period of a few months up to a year or more in which the successor begins work while overlapping with the current pastor.

This approach has great advantages but *must* have clearly articulated roles and responsibilities for each person: the exiting pastor and the arriving pastor. We work with a variety of churches developing overlap plans that vary widely depending upon the setting and circumstances.

Some churches with a long transition runway will opt to bring in a pastor who will become the senior pastor within a year or two. Caution: This is a beneficial approach but be sure the pastor who is brought in (or promoted up from within) carries a title like "senior pastor designate" so there is no confusion within the congregation.

> See "The Overlap Period" details—for the complete resource, scan the QR code or visit the companion website at the back of this book .

On-boarding can make or break a newly appointed pastor's ministry. It is vital to the culture of the church and for going forward in ministry together. While we strongly advocate for on-boarding, we urge churches to not overlook the value of in-boarding. Sometimes church leaders fall to the temptation of thinking that success in a transition is solely about the on-boarding. Both are critical and when done well, the church reaps huge rewards.

Off-boarding

Off-boarding refers to the thoughtful, intentional way a church says goodbye to its exiting pastor. It happens before the new pastor is onboarded—except during overlap periods—but simultaneous with in-boarding. It is the chance for the church to say "Thank you" and to show their appreciation; it is also the opportunity for the exiting pastor to say their thanks to the church that they have been serving.

How a church says goodbye to its exiting pastor can be as important as how it says hello to the new one. Both are opportunities to reinforce the church's culture.

Off-boarding is best done when a dedicated team is empowered with the responsibility; most of the time the off-boarding team includes various staff members who have grown close to the pastor. Typically, this team:

- listens to the goodbye hopes and expectations on the part of the pastor;
- plans and schedules significant "goodbye" events;
- arranges for the gathering of photos and other mementoes to be gifted to the pastor and family;
- produces heart-touching videos of the pastor's tenure; or
- facilitates a memorable goodbye gift to the pastor and family, often requiring some secrecy in collecting funds to achieve the element of surprise for the pastor.

Stan's goodbye included all the above, including many delightful surprises, both for Stan and for the church. For instance, Stan and his family enjoyed an amazing goodbye celebration, and in that event he surprised the church with gifts of his newly published book, Tending to a Soul.

PART THREE

Pastoral Searches: The Consultative Model

"But the Lord is the one who is marching before you! He is the one who will be with you! He won't let you down. He won't abandon you. So don't be afraid or scared!"

—Deuteronomy 31:8

Chapter 8

Preparing for a Search: Roles and Overview

Jim Ozier

In most leadership transitions, the bishop and cabinet appoint the new pastor in consultation with the church's SPRC. But we never forget Deuteronomy 31, which lifts the leadership transition from Moses to Joshua: "It is the Lord that goes before you; do not be afraid." Transitions can be fearful for the church and for the incoming pastor; there is a lot of unknown. The "system" of appointment-making is designed to help deal with the fear . . . but the spiritual reality is that as important as a system is, God's promise that the "Lord will be with us, so don't be afraid" is the undergirding of any transition system. The long history of the Wesleyan heritage and its appointment system affirms the efficacy of this approach.

A cursory look at the history of bridges reveals ancient beginnings with stones and logs laid over a swamp, through Roman stone arches, to modern structures utilizing newer technologies and techniques. The same can be said of the history of pastoral transition bridges; they evolve over time to meet the needs of the times, and at every step of that evolutionary pathway is The UMC's well-intentioned way of enabling a church to build its bridge to its future. To be sure, every iteration of a transition bridge system is built on God's promise in Deuteronomy.

That is why at specific times and for specific situations our company, Church Difference Makers, is asked to assist consultatively with identifying, recruiting, and presenting potential candidates vetted by the church to the bishop and cabinet for their consideration and appointment. In doing so, we follow our company's mantra, "Clarity-Focus-Results," as sequential steps for any project. Keep in mind too, that we *only* work for a church with the blessing of the bishop! This is what is meant by "The Consultative Model of a Pastoral Transition."

The Four Phases

There are four phases involved in building a transition bridge when it includes a pastoral search and the following chapters expand on each phase, listed below:

1. Clarity about the church's current reality *and* desired qualities in its next pastor.
2. The search itself, culminating in the bishop's appointment.
3. The Changeover Zone preparation for church and leadership.
4. Passing the baton: in-boarding, off-boarding, and onboarding.

Each phase is detailed extensively in the following chapters. The first phase, preparation that is intended to bring about clarity, is an absolute requirement to begin a pastoral search with the blessing of the bishop and is accomplished by:

- assessing the church's current reality,
- clarifying the church's needs going forward,

- discerning the church's desired qualities in their new pastor; *only* then can the church guided by its search consultant and with the blessing of the bishop even begin,
- identifying and assessing potential candidates' skill set and culture match, and
- recruiting candidates based on the above for consideration by the cabinet and SPR.

Why Current Reality Is So Important

Gil Rendle, in presenting a study to the Council of Bishops several years ago on the need to appoint pastors to larger churches in ways different from other appointments, stressed that the hardest yet most important thing is for the church to become absolutely clear about its current reality.

To read Gil Rendle's full report, scan the QR code or visit the companion website at the back of this book.

A church must dig deep into its life and gain an accurate picture of its current reality. This helps the church and also ensures that the search consultant is not presenting a less-than-candid picture to potential candidates of the true picture of the church.

But churches can also become overly self-critical, developing a distorted view of their problems and potential. A former parishioner of mine once bought his kids a pet parakeet, complete with cage, balancing stick, and mirror so the new pet would feel like it had companions. The family was so disappointed because the parakeet never sang or hopped around; it just stood in one place looking forlorn and sad. Fortunately, after several days the owner figured out the problem. The mirror in the cage was one of those two-sided types that had a regular surface on one side and a magnification surface on the other.

Inadvertently, they had placed the magnified side facing their pet. Apparently, the poor bird felt he was in the presence of a giant! When they turned the mirror around, the parakeet—responding to a more adequate reflection of itself—perked right up, living and singing a normal bird's life.

The same can be said of a church: when it fails to gain adequate self-reflection, it often responds to its challenges and context in fear and depression, sometimes to the point of paralysis. This dynamic holds true for all of us: We think we are so small, and our problems are so huge! We see the challenges staring at us bigger than they really are; we see our shortcomings larger than they are.

This mirrors what happens when a church faces a daunting pastoral transition. Many churches struggle to escape post-pandemic trends of declining worship and participation. Add to that the impact of disaffiliations and many, if not most, of our churches struggle with finances, identity, and declining influence within our respective communities.

Add into that mix the loss of a long-tenured beloved pastor and too often anxiety about the future can cause a congregation to feel as though it is up against such giant problems that they are almost paralyzed in fear and disillusionment.

But the good news is that when put in perspective, the problems we face are not bigger than the power we have as people of faith! Especially when succession planning—and for some churches a planned succession—is pursued with the commitment and intentionality that generates optimism. The Changeover Zone process proclaims, "We've got quite a song to sing!" Our Wesleyan tradition is historically one of passing the baton of leadership to meet the challenges of changing times and to leverage new ministry opportunities; of reaching the un-churched; of creating,

To access Lovers Lane's Current Reality document, scan the QR code or visit the companion website at the back of this book.

maintaining, and expanding faith communities even—and sometimes especially—during leadership transitions.

A pastoral transition is the ideal time for a church to do the hard work—research, interviews, holy conversations—of developing a written "current reality" that neither glosses over nor magnifies challenges.

Why Values Priorities Are So Important

All in all, the desired qualities articulated by either the SPRC or succession team of a church, or both, will help get at the values they hold highest. It may well be the case that no potential candidate will excel at *all* the values, skills, talents, and characteristics that a church may hope for. So this tool (available on the companion website for this book) helps the appropriate leadership teams have positive, constructive conversations that will help them (and the consultant) to gain clarity about what they are looking for. The Values Priorities tool is based on work from the Alban Institute on "Core Competencies of Larger Church Leadership" by Susan Beaumont. It helps bring some clarity for the local church utilizing the common language expressed by most bishops regarding leadership competencies. It includes such elements as preaching and worship and range to spiritual maturity and decision-making.

To access the complete Leadership Case Statement tool and a sample survey, scan the QR code or visit the companion website at the back of this book.

Why "Needs Going Forward" Is So Important

Gaining clarity on the church's current reality, desired qualities in its next pastor, on what needs the church feels it needs to address is critical when a church begins a pastoral search. Clarity on these keeps the SPRC and succession team from chasing rabbits, wasting time, or getting unduly confused. We approach getting clarity with this final pre-search tool designed to (1) present the church's case to the bishop and district superintendent for their approval and input, (2) make sure the search consultant is armed with accurate information, and (3) assist the succession team and the SPRC in having healthy conversations with each other as the search goes forward.

As part of the pre-search tool we also offer a Leadership Case Statement resource to be completed by the appropriate staff/laity for the consultant's use in putting together the church's "case" that is shared both with candidates and the bishop's office. We are often asked about the wisdom of an all church survey to help prepare the case statement. While we don't usually recommend this because it can create more anxiety than clarity, if your church is considering such a step, take a look at the resources we make available.

The Role of the Current Pastor in Building the Bridge

What is the appropriate role of the current pastor during the transition? This question can make or break a transition—its impact runs deep. During the transition, the pastor must lead with a calming hand (there is always lots of anxiety, especially among staff), always reassuring all audiences that a well-thought-out plan is guiding the transition. The pastor should never utter a negative word about the bishop, the church, or the transition bridge-building process. A pastor's—or any leader's—negative word, when repeated, becomes a sentence; repeated further, a paragraph; repeated more, a page. You get the idea. A wise pastor includes teaching moments during sermons explaining our biblical understanding of "being sent," which is the basis for our appointment system; a helpful pastor will constantly cheerlead and express thanks to all involved in the transition; an effective pastor will not be perceived as coasting downhill as their tenure comes to an end, but will be heralded as claiming a last hurrah in which ministry is led forward in an exciting fashion!

The current pastor's role in the search process, however, should be carefully weighed, clearly carried out, and deliberately limited. Our experience is that it is a mistake to completely remove the current pastor from the search process. It is equally a mistake to overly involve the exiting pastor in deliberations about who the successor should be. Skeptics will often suggest the pastor is "picking their successor," which would be detrimental to the entire process.

Pastoral Succession Chaos: Ripped from the Headlines

A real-life drama of succession not done well and the resultant chaos when a retiring senior pastor hand-picked his own successor played out in 2025 in Houston, Texas. According to an article in the Houston Chronicle entitled, "What to know about second Baptist church, a 98 year old Houston megachurch being sued by its members, "For fifty years, Rev. Ed Young led the famed, ninety-eight-year-old Houston Second Baptist Church—boasting over ninety-four thousand congregants, $1 billion in assets, and high-profile members. But on May 26, 2024, Young stepped down and named his son, Rev. Ben Young, as his successor.

Seems simple and straightforward? Not quite. According to reports from constituents and legal filings, "The church is at war with its own members." A large and influential group within the congregation filed suit claiming the church had fraudulently passed bylaws behind closed doors that allowed Young to personally name his son as successor, and stripped members of their voting rights.[1]

Admittedly, this was a particularly bitter episode, and it happened within an ecclesiological system totally alien to The UMC. Still, it leaves a troubling impression throughout the church world. And there are many other examples where chaos reigns when a senior pastor names his or her own successor in a display of control and power. It can be argued that a long-tenured retiring pastor in fact knows more about the church, its culture and needs, and the community than anybody else, and therefore should have the deciding voice about the successor. But the argument breaks down in the light of the reality that the retiring pastor's vision for the future is often clouded by deeply entrenched blind spots of the church's current condition and perceived needs to meet a new future. Without checks and balances, insight sharing, and deliberations that capture diverse perspectives, the temptation can be overwhelming to pick a successor that simply reflects the current pastor.

There is an appropriate role for the current pastor that balances (a) the extensive knowledge and corporate memory long-tenured pastors hold about their church, with (b) the need to avoid any appearance of choosing or unduly influencing the successor.

Throughout the transition, the current pastor has one last and essential part to play: the role of cheerleader. No one is better positioned to publicly bless the work of the SPRC and succession team. As we have mentioned, there is an ever-present anxiety when there is a change of pastors. That is why it is so important for the current pastor to be 100 percent positive and supportive of the process and the new successor, especially with staff and key leaders—but also throughout the congregation, conference, and community.

There is also an appropriate role for the current pastor during the "preparation" phase. While the succession team and SPRC gathers information about current reality, needs going forward, and desired qualities in the next pastor, they benefit greatly from hearing the current pastor's perspective. At Lovers Lane, Stan was asked to prepare from his heart a summarizing document reflecting his twenty-seven-year tenure, which could be shared with the Succession Team/SPRC. This is what he wrote:

As I See It

In sharing what I see needed in a new lead pastor I share this reflection and will first raise the question, is it still a value in a senior pastor to be looking for someone who is drawn to Lovers Lane's uniqueness, is aware of the challenges posed by diversity, and is ready to face this somewhat-complicated congregation? There will always be significant challenges in such a church as

Lovers Lane. Someone chosen with rose-colored glasses about this being a cushy, prestigious place to be will likely see the error of their choice in coming. The ministry here is work, and hard work will be required.

Also, a "rising star" who is young and energetic is not a negative by any means, but that is not the only profile that would work well. Our model of multiple community/campus pastors lessens the negative impact of a lead pastor replacement and broadens the age-level appeal. Certainly, being white and male is not a must, and may not even be any kind of advantage. That is not to say that a white male clergy should be ruled out by any means, but it is to say being open to female leadership, and non-Anglo clergy is an appropriate and just consideration.

NOTE: Lovers Lane has a very female-led and diverse staff compared to most other large United Methodist churches. There are six female and five male clergy presently. If a female lead pastor is chosen, focus on new associate pastoral appointments being male may need to be a priority. Now that is different!

A senior pastor has to be comfortable in sharing management of staff, pulpit time with other pastors, as well as pastoral care responsibilities with other staff members. It requires a strength of character, degree of trust, and not being threatened by sharing responsibility and power with other loyal staff members. I had to grow into this stance and a new pastor will be advised to do the same. Therefore, building relationships with staff members and loving and caring for them, being their pastor is more of a requirement than the ability to manage them. This is different, but it works well and acceptance of this approach would be necessary to avoid major disruption.

The new lead pastor needs to have good experience and a good record with growing a church and the principles of evangelism. Growth, and growing younger as a congregation, is a need, and the age of the new pastor does impact the age-related growth. The congregation will typically grow in the service related to the age of the lead pastor. The growth will likely be ten years younger and up to fifteen years older than the lead pastor. I.e., a forty-year-old pastor will see growth of 30somethings up to mid-fiftysome-things. Also, remember the ages of the other lead worship pastors determines the age of growth in those services. Our services led by younger pastors than I are getting younger than the congregational average age.

The new senior pastor will have a big job ahead. But the good news is, she or he won't be carrying the weight alone. Lovers Lane has a talented group of lay leaders and boards who are committed to finding creative solutions. It's not just about raising money, it's about building relationships and working together to ensure that our church, and all the ministries we support, continue to thrive.

NOTE: It is a misnomer to believe that our capital campaigns were magically successful because we followed some cookie-cutter fundraising approach led by a company hired to do the work. The truth is that our staff, our leadership, and the people of Lovers Lane are astute fundraisers, and we've raised approximately $55 million through campaigns for buildings and endowments. It's not been easy, but it's what has been done together. The preceding information was solicited by the Church Difference Makers consultant and was part of a larger piece titled, "As I see It," by Stanley R. Copeland, senior pastor, Lovers Lane UMC 1998–2025.

The first phase is essential before candidates enter into any conversations. There is an important distinction between a "candidate" and a "prospect." The consultant may actually begin looking for "prospects" while the clarity information is being developed to share with prospects who become candidates. Equally important is clarity on the following items, which don't require the hard work of research and preparing documents, but they do require the hard work of consensus within the church leadership and the bishop's blessing:

1. when to consider a pastoral search,
2. why consider a pastoral search, and
3. the role of the consultant in a pastoral search.

When to Consider a Pastoral Search

While every church could benefit from Changeover Zone training, not every church is suited to—or needs—a consultant-led search. Typically, larger churches with multiple staff, complex systems, and diverse membership benefit the most from a consultative model of pastoral searches.

Bishops tend to contact us in situations where a church deemed mission-critical is facing severe trauma, conflict, or broken trust relationships internally or with the "system"

Churches tend to contact us when their current long-term pastor is retiring, and when the church displays a unique, complex culture that leadership perceives needs a wide pool of candidates who may become the successor. In either case our role is to partner with and assist the bishop and cabinet, not to replace them. Having served on a cabinet for seven years, I appreciate the difficulties cabinets must navigate. So we are committed to keeping all parties constantly up to date with the sequential stages of our work and follow all protocols the bishop expects.

Why Do a Pastoral Search

A pastoral search done in the consultative model provides added value not only for the church but also for the bishop and cabinet. Here are a few values:

1. Many churches carry a perception of having been "wronged" by the cabinet: "What if's" and "Why us?" laments abound

in some SPRCs, passed down from generation to generation. Bishops tend to contact us about transitions where there is a perception that trust has eroded. The search model provides an approach where churches perceive they have more of a voice, while at the same time we are committed to teaching SPRCs about the work of the cabinet system in a positive way.

2. Often in a church's "current reality" there are hidden landmines that stressed-out, stretched-thin district superintendents going through conference and district realignments may not readily pick up on. From my years as both a large church pastor and an appointive cabinet member I have seen how the attention of many superintendents faces the gravitational pull of "putting out fires" among many of their churches. Our process expands their bandwidth to dig deeper into the church's current reality and its needs in a new pastor.
3. Pastors strive to put top-notch members on the SPRC, often with either human resource backgrounds or experience in leading business and other corporate ventures, or both. These members speak the language of consultants; and there seems to be a growing number of members who themselves are consultants in their respective fields. Utilizing a consultant makes sense to them and lends itself to respecting the process and feeling like they are a part of a positive approach to securing leadership.
4. The consultative model envisioned by church strategist Gil Rendle in a report to the Council of Bishops is designed for larger churches with more complex systems. Even though superintendents and bishops have a wealth of church experience and wisdom, often they do not have firsthand larger church pastoral experience. All of our trained consultants in planned succession and pastoral searches have been successful long-tenured large church pastors themselves. The "been there, done that" dynamic lends credibility to the SPRC.
5. Our role is to partner with the bishop and cabinet, not to substitute for them. We are committed to following all the bishop's

protocols and to consistently promote their value to churches with whom we work.

The Role of the Consultant in a Pastoral Search

At Church Difference Makers, all our search consultants are well-trained, retired UMC clergy with successful experience pastoring larger churches with multiple staff. I (Jim Ozier) either lead a search or supervise other team members when they are assisting a church and the bishop in conducting a search. A search consultant working with a church and with the blessing of the bishop has a clearly defined role that is communicated up front to church leadership as they discern whether to contract for our services.

The concept of pastoral search consultants is relatively new in United Methodism and there is often confusion, skepticism, resistance, and even ridicule about it. I have served as a search consultant since 2017 and have helped secure—with the blessing of and in partnership with the resident bishop—the pastoral leadership of many of the largest churches in the denomination. Despite receiving countless emails of affirmation and appreciation from pastors, church members, and bishops who are ecstatic about the results of our work, we occasionally still face pushback and objections to what we do.

So, to clarify, here is the *role of a consultant* in a pastoral search:

1. The consultant leverages their successful experience as a large church pastor to guide a church through the transition process. Many churches are going through a transition for the first time in a long time. They simply don't know what to do. We go through pastoral transitions repeatedly.
2. The consultants guide the church leadership in completing all the pre-search work of current reality, values priorities, and the case study—but we do not do the work ourselves.
    a. We do not formulate a church's current reality; the church does.

  b. We do not suggest what a church needs going forward; the church does.

  c. We do not tell a church what it should desire in its next pastor; the church does.

3. The consultant may offer insights, point out obstacles to overcome, or point out potential landmines to navigate in facilitating a successful pastoral transition.

4. The consultant identifies and presents prospects in the search to the SPRC.

5. The consultant does not decide which prospects will become "candidates"; the SPRC team, in conjunction with the bishop, does. The consultant rarely even participates in any interviews because we feel this is "family business" to be done by the church leadership itself.

6. The consultant does not decide who among candidates becomes a finalist to present to the bishop for consideration; the SPRC team decides.

7. The consultant does not select the church's new pastor; only the bishop appoints their new pastor.

8. The consultant keeps the bishop aware of every step of the search, including names the SPRC team recommends considering as candidates.

9. The consultant communicates to the team if, for any reason, the bishop eliminates any potential candidate from consideration.

10. The consultant does not speak to a prospect or candidate's bishop if they come from outside the conference; only the resident bishop speaks to another bishop.

11. The consultant always speaks to the team positively and with affirmation of the bishop and any actions the bishop takes.

12. The consultant does not advocate to the bishop about who should be appointed as the church's next pastor; the SPRC chairperson and the bishop engage in those conversations.

13. The consultant may negotiate logistical issues with candidate finalists, where appropriate and approved by the bishop.

14. The consultant—after the bishop has appointed the new pastor—does guide the church through its next transition functions:
    a. In-boarding (after announcement but prior to arrival) of the new pastor,
    b. Off-boarding of the exiting pastor, and
    c. On-boarding (after arrival of new pastor through first 12 months).
15. The consultant works only with the bishop's blessing and partnership.

Chapter 9

Conducting a Pastoral Search

Jim Ozier

Jesus said, "Follow me, . . . and I'll show you how to fish for people" (Matthew 4:19). A pastoral search is fishing for the right pastor to lead a congregation that fishes for new people. Chapter 8 covered clarity—the essential first phase. Now we move to phase 2: the search itself. In this phase the succession team (1) identifies and assesses prospects' skill sets and culture fit, and (2) recruits candidates to present to the bishop, cabinet, and SPRC.

Both "identifying" and "recruiting" came into play for the Lovers Lane transition. When Eddie Rester's name first surfaced, no one around Lovers Lane had even heard of him—nor had I as the consultant. But over a three-month period, after great intentionality and excitement, Dr. Eddie Rester was appointed to become Stan Copeland's successor. Here is just a bit of the search process from Eddie's perspective:

I was first contacted about Lovers Lane during Jim Ozier's sonar search. As a pastor who became involved in the search process, I felt I had consistent access to clear and helpful information every step of the way. The work of Church Difference Makers also gave the church an opportunity to tell its story in an honest, compelling way that helped prepare me for going through all the stages of the search: from a prospect, to a candidate, to a finalist, and finally being presented to Bishop Saenz for his discernment, before appointing as this wonderful church's next senior pastor. All throughout the various junctures of the exhaustive process, I was able to have meaningful conversations with the SPRC's search team. At the same time, Bishop Saenz was able to have similar conversations with my bishop in Mississippi.

Most important, the slow and intentional nature of the process created space for discernment. It allowed me to listen for how God was moving in my life and in my family's life. As my wife, Audra, and I considered a move to a new city and state, having that time to pray and reflect together as a family was deeply important.

After the search was finalized, Lovers Lane's staff and leadership provided a thoughtful transition plan to ensure a seamless handoff from Stan to me. Beyond transferring information, it created space for a healthy transfer of pastoral authority and trust—a gift that made the transition not only smooth but also spiritually grounded.

Each key player has a specific role in building the transition bridge. But take great care: overlooked details can collapse even the most worthy goal. Such was the case of the collapse of the Truesdell Bridge in Dixon, Illinois, in 1873 when it was overloaded with onlookers observing a baptism ceremony. Considered the worst road bridge disaster in American history, forty-six people were killed and fifty-six injured. Engineers determined the cause was flawed design and inadequate materials; the builders had simply overlooked the details.

When a transition becomes merely a transaction rather than a transformation, we build a flawed bridge vulnerable to collapse—even in the most sacred times. When a pastoral search is involved, every detail in design and execution becomes critical. Conducting a pastoral search with the bishop's blessing requires preparation well before the search begins. Overlooking the smallest of preparation details can prove disastrous, as can taking shortcuts in the design of the search process. Key roles drive accountability and success. We've already shared the roles of consultant and exiting pastor in building the transition bridge. Below is a summary of the other, equally important key role.

The Role of Church Leadership in a Pastoral Search

- Typically, the resident bishop grants a local church permission to contract with Church Difference Makers for a consultant-model pastoral search.

- The pastor and SPRC often recruit a high-capacity group of church members to form a succession or search team. The search team usually consists of several members of the SPRC plus other leadership influencers. In some settings the SPRC does not involve a "succession" or "search" team, but handles all those responsibilities itself.

- Works (as in the case with Lovers Lane) directly with the consultant and reported to the SPRC. Its functions included (a) developing the church's current reality and values priority with input from appropriate leadership groups and the current pastor. This function created the church's case statement to be shared with prospects and candidates, (b) providing assessed potential prospects and candidates based on the Leadership Case Statement, (c) ensuring a consistent communication strategy to keep the congregation in the loop and up to date, (d) agreeing, in conjunction with the SPRC and the consultant, on the logistics to recruit potential candidates for the purpose of securing the successor to their exiting pastor, and (e) arriving through the process with one to three finalists, which it presented to the bishop for consideration and appointment as the new pastor.

- Coordinates church-related logistics like moving expenses, for enabling the bishop's appointed pastor to hit the ground running.

- Works to maintain confidentiality, which is paramount. Throughout the search, church leaders must work together positively and productively. Multiple meetings on sensitive subjects must create space for diverse perspectives to be expressed in a healthy and safe way.

To review the "Working Together Agreement" on confidentiality, scan the QR code or visit the companion website at the back of this book.

The Five Foundations of Phase 2: The Search Itself

1. Only the resident bishop can make an appointment.
2. If a potential candidate emerges out-of-conference, the resident bishop will contact and receive permission from the prospective candidate's bishop before he or she will be considered a candidate.
3. Maintaining candidate confidentiality is our highest priority.
4. The consultant, search team, and SPRC work in partnership with the bishop and cabinet.

5. To ease congregation anxiety during transition, keep the congregation and staff updated regularly on all public aspects of the search through creative, transparent communication.

Sources of Prospects and Potential Candidates

Usually for a local church pastoral search, there are four sources of candidates:

1. **Internal:** These are effective and beloved staff members of the searching church. They may ask to be considered as prospects for the lead pastor position. Often such staff members have enthusiastic cheerleaders advocating for them, but they must still go through the search process to become considered as candidates.
2. **External:** Usually these are pastors from the church's district or conference lifted by friends and they share dynamics similar to internal candidates.
3. **Expanded:** This begins with the sonar search and may be regional or nationwide. These pastors are subject to all aspects of a search as described in the process.
4. **Cabinet:** These are pastors whom the cabinet would be considering, even if the church was not utilizing the consultant model of a pastoral search. The cabinet generally shares these names with the consultant or with the chair of the search team.

Overview of the Search Process

A pastoral search has three sequential, connected steps: (1) the sonar search, (2) the prospect search, and (3) the candidate search. These steps form the basis of a pastoral search, done with the resident bishop's blessing in conjunction with a church undergoing pastoral transition. Sometimes the local church contracts with us; other times the bishop or a district superintendent does. Our process is the same either way. Below is a short summary of the steps:

For complete details—including overview, sonar search, prospect search, and candidate search—scan the QR code or visit the companion website at the back of this book.

1. **Sonar Search:** The consultant begins fishing by casting a wide net through networking with colleagues to lift up names of pastors who may possibly match the ministry needs of a church of a particular size and complexity. If the church or bishop has announced a change, the church is identified in the sonar search. If the church has not publicly announced its intentions, then the sonar search is done with no identifiers, just a generic description like "a large progressive church in the Midwest" for example. It resembles brainstorming possible candidates. This often begins before the church completes compiling its case statement and values priorities for prospects. Sonar search names may come also from church members, district superintendents, and so on. Typically, less than 50 percent of names will become actual prospects.

For a sample sonar search letter to colleagues, scan the QR code or visit the companion website at the back of this book.

2. **Prospect Search:** The consultant reflects on sonar search names and needs of the church. The consultant will have conversations with any prospective candidates. When pastors choose to be

considered a prospective candidate and the consultant agrees, their name will be given to the resident bishop, who in turn may share with the prospect's bishop, stressing the importance of confidentiality in this early stage of the process. Typically, less than 60 percent of prospects will be invited to and will agree to become candidates.

3. **Candidate Search:** The search narrows prospects to candidates by examining data, third-party input, and church values, with the resident bishop's approval.

NOTE: Pastors *only* become candidates when they inform the consultant they would like to be considered as a candidate, the search team invites them to be a candidate, and *after* the resident bishop blesses their candidacy. Their candidacy is not public, and we strive for complete confidentiality. Typically, the candidate search narrows through vetting and interviews to one to three finalists. If a potential candidate is out-of-conference, the resident bishop will do due diligence. The potential prospect for candidacy should initiate appropriate conversations with either their district superintendent or bishop, or both. Remember that all the above is only part of the journey toward church selection of a new pastor; no assumption should be made as to being selected for appointment.

Following the Bishop's Protocols

The local church involved in a pastoral transition is proud to be part of a connectional system. Thus, the consultant ensures the church maintains good faith with the resident bishop. Therefore, the bishop will set the protocols and methods for how the search team will assess candidates and arrive at finalists (usually one to three) for consideration.

- For clarity, the consultant will provide the search team written protocols from the bishop regarding ways and means to assess candidates (résumés, references, virtual conversations, in-person or consultant interviews, worship experiences, etc.).

- At some point the bishop will likely interview or be a part of finalist interviews with the search team. Remember that only the bishop will make the appointment.

- Some bishops prefer the SPRC to arrive at finalists to present to the bishop for her or his discernment and appointive action. Other bishops prefer the consultant present the bishop with the top candidates for episcopal and cabinet discernment, who then works with the SPRC in finalizing the appointment.

- Either way, it is anticipated that deciding on finalists and receiving an appointment as the new lead pastor will be a Holy Spirit–led venture. In searches there are often diverse and divergent opinions by decision makers, so we encourage prayerful and grace-filled discernment and attitudes to come to consensus.

Church Difference Maker Research Early in the Process

When a name emerges, we begin basic research to determine whether that pastor might become a prospect. One of our trusted team members researches the pastor's church website, social media, and personal profile. (If, for instance, we know the church for whom we are searching is progressive and inclusive but the possible prospect is very traditional and uses language that wouldn't fit into our client's culture, then we remove that pastor from the client church's possibility list.) This step narrows the list to names of folks who may become prospects.

The Difference Between a "Prospect" and a "Candidate"

A "prospect" is someone who: (1) represents and displays the highest ideals of Jesus Christ and United Methodism; (2) has a high degree of skill set, character, and cultural affinity that will likely match the church's expressed needs; (3) leads the church and the consultant to agree he or she could likely become a candidate representing the right kind of pastor the church desires; and (4) is prayerfully willing to engage with the church in a deeper way and will confide in their own bishop or superintendent an interest in exploring the possibility of becoming a candidate.

A "candidate" is someone who, in addition to the above, (1) meets the church's requirements and is willing to enter into discernment about being the "right" person to lead the church into the future; (2) is willing and eager to fully engage in the discernment process, including agreeing to any church-required background checks and deeper vetting; and (3) would be given permission to be appointed by the resident bishop and his or her own bishop if from another conference.

A word about how and when a prospect's information is shared with the church and the resident bishop is summarized in the following steps:

- If pastors choose to be considered a "prospect," they will have conversations with the consultant about the church and about themselves, as well as provide a résumé to the consultant. The consultant will turn the résumé into a profile without identifiers indicating name, current appointment, or geographical location.

- The consultant will structure the profile details by his or her sense for what elements will indicate a strong, medium, or unknown match to the church's expressed needs, complexities, and culture. An unknown match is not negative; it just indicates more information is needed.

- The church's SPRC or search team will review all profiles presented by the consultant, and make one of three responses and prioritize them based on (1) we definitely would like to learn more about this person; (2) let's hold off on that person for a while, but we may be interested in the future; (c) this sounds like a good pastor but not necessarily a good match for us.

- If the church requests more information, the consultant will contact the pastor and ask if their name, résumé, and more information can be shared confidentially with the committee. If yes, the pastor becomes a "candidate" for the position, and we proceed; if no, the consultant will assume the pastor does not feel confident declaring himself or herself as a candidate.

NOTE: Bishop-to-bishop protocols deserve delicate and respectful timing when it comes to out-of-conference pastors who may become prospects or candidates. When a résumé is requested or received, the consultant will share the name with the resident bishop, but not yet with the SPRC or search team. Bishop-to-bishop conversations then will occur that may influence the process accordingly.

Once pastors become prospects, they receive regular updates on all search aspects.

- A prospect's identifiers will only be shared with a church with their permission.

- A pastor will only be considered a candidate when they tell the consultant that is their desire, and the church agrees and after they have spoken with either their district superintendent or bishop, or both.

For the Pastoral Prospect Assessment Questions, scan the QR code or visit the companion website at the back of this book.

Note: It is not unusual for the "prospect list" that our team considers to include between twenty to thirty names, depending on the size and the stature of a searching church.

The Candidate Search

By the time the search identifies viable candidates, the team has invested hundreds of hours. By this time, the consultant actively seeks input from the bishop and district superintendent on possible candidates. It is not uncommon that the church's search has lifted up the name of some pastor somewhere and either (a) the resident bishop has removed a potential prospect or candidate from consideration for reasons that perhaps only the bishop knows; or (b) the bishop of a prospect in another conference—after conversation with that prospect's bishop—has removed them from further consideration. The search team understands these possibilities and has agreed to honor the bishop's decisions. It is important to honor the bishop's protocols on this key determination: Will members of the SPRC/Succession/Search team be allowed to go on-site to a candidate's church to assess them? Or may the SPRC bring a candidate to the church for further vetting?

For guideline questions to assess a candidate in a worship setting, scan the QR code or visit the companion website at the back of this book.

Defining a Candidate

A "candidate" is someone who, beyond prospect requirements, (1) meets the church's requirements and will engage in deeper conversations about leading the church forward; (2) will fully participate in the discernment process, including background checks; and (3) has approval from the resident bishop and their own bishop if from another conference.

Candidates provide their full résumé to the succession/search team with the understanding that it remains confidential to the team and bishop at this stage. Candidate confidentiality remains our highest value.

As candidates progress through assessments and interviews, search teams track their advancement using language such as the following to identify finalists for the bishop:

- good candidates (typically between 10–15),
- top-tier candidates (typically between 5–10), and
- finalists (usually between 1–3).

The Relationship Between Candidates and the Search Team

Multiple candidates typically emerge for lead pastor consideration. Every candidate will have proven themself a great communicator, skilled pastor, and accomplished leader. Likely, any finalist for a large, nationally known church could serve most churches in the Connection. The search team seeks not the best candidate but the right candidate who is the best match for the church.

While the SPRC team is assessing candidates, candidates are assessing the church. The SPRC understands they're also recruiting the candidate's family—especially if the candidate would be relocating. *Preparing an individual recruitment strategy with the SPRC addresses each finalist's needs and expectations.* The strategy will:

- encompass and allow for ways in which the candidate can do their due diligence in learning as much about the church as possible, including its staff and leadership, ministries and practices, and its culture;

- clarify compensation considerations, moving expenses, benefits, and other logistics; and
- include family considerations such as housing, spousal employment, childcare, and school situations if applicable.

Note: Input from the retiring pastor can provide valuable insight into this aspect of the search process. The retiring pastor won't serve on the search team or participate in interviews, but may meet with top candidates if the candidates request it.

As Stan has shared, often those who become candidates—especially finalists—like to learn more about "the real scoop" of the church, and they like to hear it from the retiring pastor. The long-tenured pastor has deep perspective on how the church's various parts function together. The consultant arranges such visits virtually (usually) or in person (occasionally), unless the bishop's protocols prevent it.

Finalist Search

How does a candidate become a finalist when the initial pool may include more than fifty names? The sonar search uncovers possible names, and we solicit additional names from internal candidates, church members, team suggestions, and self-nominations.

As we compile possibilities, our online researcher examines websites and social media. Another researcher reviews online sermons and offers evaluations. You may wonder why we vet candidates this way initially. We want to ensure our consultants don't favor a particular candidate and lose objectivity. Before someone becomes a finalist,

For Lovers Lane's interview questions, scan the QR code or visit the companion website at the back of this book.

at least three Church Difference Makers staff members participate in observations.

Rest assured, the SPRC/search/succession team's observations carry more weight than ours. Recall: the team initially evaluates anonymous profiles prepared by the consultant with no identifiers. Once the team wants to learn more, they ask if that person would like to become a candidate. Then things accelerate, usually starting with virtual interviews, followed by one or more in-person interviews. Team members use a common set of questions to ensure fair comparisons.

After intense, prayerful meetings, consensus develops on the three finalists to present to the bishop. Some teams prioritize the three finalists; others don't. It depends on the bishop's instructions. A "finalist" is a pastor who can meet the church's identified needs, possesses desired skills and pastoral spirit, and displays essential character and culture alignment. When the team presents three finalists, they've concluded any of the three would be an excellent fit. They leave it to the bishop's discernment to decide which of the three will be appointed. If the team has prioritized finalists, members covenant to fully support the bishop's choice—no second-guessing, no complaints, no undermining.

The consultant personally contacts each finalist not selected by the bishop. After selection, the consultant contacts all other prospects and candidates involved in the search. We seek to strengthen UMC appointment culture through the courtesy of personally informing all involved.

By the finalist stage, it's clear all finalists are strong pastors and leaders. The question for the team then is not, "Who is the best candidate?" but "Who is the right candidate for us?" To answer this, they spend considerable time discussing the subtle differences among finalists.

The Seven Significant Separators

The SPRC or succession teams assess wonderful pastors by evaluating their vision-casting and leadership abilities. Routinely, they also evaluate problem-solving and conflict resolution skills.

For the "Significant Seven Separators" conversation starter tool, scan the QR code or visit the companion website at the back of this book.

These high-level questions elevate a pastor to legitimate "candidate" status. But in moving a candidate into becoming a "finalist" the team must diligently consider the framing questions to guide decisions of (a) Who becomes a finalist? (b) What values and desired preferences move a candidate into the finalist list? (c) What weight does the team place on the typically "Significant Seven Separators" for their church at this time to elevate someone into the coveted position of being a finalist?

- church fit
- experience
- preaching
- relatability
- staff management
- missional outreach
- what do they bring to us?

While all are important, their weight varies by church situation. The tool is designed to ask, ***Which of the above bears greater importance to what the church needs for its next lead pastor, and why?***

Scanning the Horizon

In rarer cases, the succession process begins discreetly three to five years before the transition. For transitions planned three to five years out due to planned retirement, we use a technique of "Scanning the Horizon." Though still uncommon, these longer-runway situations are beginning to occur more frequently. This process recognizes that there are unique churches whose size, complexity, influence, and needs require advance planning to even begin saying goodbye to a beloved, long-tenured pastor, and hello to a successor with enormous challenges and opportunities in front of them. These situations require trust and candid conversations between the resident bishop and church leadership.

Context

Before setting out, anglers scan the horizon for signs of what the fishing trip may bring. Swirls indicate fish are moving, diving birds suggest fish are feeding, and storm clouds signal the need to adjust plans.

Church leadership often recognizes the need to scan the horizon before seeking successors to a beloved pastor contemplating retirement within three to five years. Advanced planning is essential for many large, complex churches. Some must prepare for possibly the largest transition in their history over multiple years while minimizing anxiety and rumors. Such transitions are unprecedented in scope for many individual churches and conferences. This requires flexibility, creativity, and mutual trust.

Horizon Planning

Any far-in-advance planning must protect confidentiality throughout the three-to-five-year runway. It covers the time window preceding our typical sonar search and is designed to assist the church to scan—with the full blessing of the bishop—the distant horizon as they prepare to begin fishing for a successor to a long-tenured (and sometimes also founding) pastor of a larger church.

Engagement with a Consultant

Taking into account the long runway (up to five years) leading to a unique pastoral transition, any arrangements with the consultant are made with the full agreement of the resident bishop and with the understanding that throughout the long runway, the church's various search-related committees will monitor progress and needs. At this point, they may or may not elect to enter into additional agreements with Church Difference Makers related to the pastoral search.

Requirements of any Scanning-the-Horizon Arrangement

To avoid anxiety and rumors, pastors identified in scanning the horizon remain confidential and unaware of their inclusion. To avoid awkwardness and protect confidentiality, the church and consultant observe potential candidates' ministry progress from a distance. These observations may later lead the church to consider specific pastors as prospects when the search begins.

PART FOUR

Building a Successful Transition Bridge

Take the things you heard me say in front of many other witnesses and pass them on to faithful people who are also capable of teaching others.

—2 Timothy 2:2

Chapter 10

Preparing for a Great Transition

Jim Ozier

As we move to phase 3 of the four phases—the Changeover Zone—it is important to approach it like the popular commercial: "Just OK is not OK"! A great transition is more than smooth execution—it's a "marker moment" that increases the church's growth potential. Few moments offer better growth potential than a well-executed pastoral transition.

When a church learns of an impending pastoral change, it enters the Changeover Zone. Usually, the church enters the Changeover Zone months before the new pastor is named. This period provides critical time for intentional preparation of the congregation. A fast-paced series of events unfolds seamlessly, resulting in a successful passing of the baton. Whether it is a planned succession or a more typical pastoral transition, it requires succession planning and preparation. The various participants—pastors, church, and supervisors—design and execute preplanned, prepared actions carried out with the precision of a successful team! Ideally, the Changeover Zone covers the one hundred days before new pastors arrive, and the one hundred days after new pastors have begun.

Changeover Zone Workshops for a Church

Ideally, church leadership schedules a Changeover Zone Workshop approximately one hundred days before the current pastor retires. This interactive workshop should be extensively publicized and carefully prepared. Make it a big deal! Often—but not always—a church knows the name of its newly appointed pastor, and occasionally their new pastor may even be able to be present. We have already spoken about the Changeover Zone, but the following is related to the all-important church workshop.

- Who should attend? Definitely the church leadership. To strengthen the church's culture, we recommend opening it to all church members.
- The workshop explains every role in creating a great transition and develops a written course of action for saying goodbye to the current pastor and welcoming the new pastor.
- What should be the set up? The workshop typically runs three to four hours. Some churches prefer a morning session (9 a.m.–12 p.m.); some prefer an afternoon (1 p.m.–4 p.m.). Some like to include a meal (10 a.m.–2 p.m.). Media should be available, as best-practice example videos are used throughout. Seating at round tables facilitates smaller-group discussion.

Modules in this workshop cover (a) preparing the local church, (b) preparing the exiting pastor for a strong handoff, and (c) preparing the arriving pastor for a fast start.

Changeover Zone Workshops for Conferences

The above approach is typical for local churches. However, we often conduct Changeover Zone workshops for annual conferences. The Northern Illinois Conference, for example, designs its yearly event as a required training for all their pastors who will be moving, together with the respective SPRC chairs of churches going through a transition. Most conference district superintendents also participate. It is a five-hour-long event typically held on a Saturday. Two additional virtual sessions accommodate clergy and SPRC chairs who miss the in-person event. All workshops include extensive workbooks (clergy and local church versions) covering all material and additional resources.

Whether on-site or online, we pledge to stay on target. How long should a local church's Changeover Zone last? It depends.

- Is your church going through a more or less traditional pastoral transition that it often goes through about every three to four years?
- Is your church going through a long-tenured transition in which a longer-tenured pastor is saying goodbye through retirement or receiving a new appointment? Or has it been a long time since you've had a pastoral transition?
- Is your church suffering through what might be called "a burning platform," which indicates some kind of imminent crisis or troubled waters? There has to be a change!
- Are you in a new church plant going through its first pastoral change? The change may be coming after a few years. Or even if it is after many years, perhaps the church hasn't gone through it before.

Changeover Zone preparation is not about the appointment being made. It does not depend on how the appointment is made—whether by the bishop and cabinet or planned succession with their blessing. Changeover Zone preparation acknowledges the church's intentional role in building a positive transition bridge to its future.

The world has changed, and so has the church. Detailed preparation enables churches not only to pass the baton smoothly but also to grow through transition. How the baton is passed shapes church culture and creates excitement. This book has been about exploring ways to change pastoral transition approaches that benefit the UMC system and examining effective ways to prepare churches and pastors for a strong baton pass.

In the then–North Texas Conference (now Horizon Texas) every few years we would conduct annual conference away from the Dallas area and in the vibrant smaller city of Wichita Falls. I still remember the year delegates were greeted by the mayor of the city and a UMC church member, Mr. Charles Harper, with this story: "When I graduated from college," said Mr. Harper in his captivating style, "my father took me aside at the family gathering and presented me with a gift. An axe. This is the same axe that my grandfather gave to my father when he graduated from college," explained Charles, "and your grandfather's father gave to him; and your great-great grandfather gave to him when he became a young man. The same axe your great-great-great-grandfather used to clear the ground when he homesteaded in Wichita Falls."

Charles told attendees that he was a young guy full of vinegar and skeptically questioned his dad: "You mean to tell me this is the very same axe that my great-great-great grandfather actually used to work the land?" Charles then said his father gave him lasting words of wisdom: "Well, son, over the years it has had a few different heads, and a few different handles . . . but it is the same axe!"

It's not an axe we're handing off. It's a baton—leadership passed from one pastor to another. Over the years, through many changes, it has had a few different handles and a few different heads . . . but it is the same baton that Jesus handed to Peter and said, "I'll build my church on this rock" (Matthew 16:18).

How the baton is passed sustains United Methodist culture—it's a sacred act with deep historical roots. It's fine that the passing of the baton has evolved; it's still the same baton. It's not a simple transaction. It's a sacred relationship that endures and adapts when executed well.

We offer workshops online for churches, conferences, districts, and more. We also provide a complimentary one-hour follow-up consultation for churches that attend our on-site workshops to address their specific needs. Budget-conscious conferences often choose all-virtual formats. Virtual events are good but they lack a critical workshop goal: mitigating anxiety. And there is often anxiety at a workshop on the part of the SPRC, with themes of "Our church is already angry about the transition" or "We don't know anything about the next pastor," and so on.

An on-site event mitigates anxiety and magnifies excitement through group dynamics, humor, engagement, and live interaction.

Virtual conversations deliver information, but live messaging is far more effective. Virtual settings often increase anxiety among participants who feel isolated. Unfortunately, the back-and-forth banter and laughter of a live workshop seldom translates as well as we would like in a virtual setting.

For examples from Lovers Lane's Passing the Baton Sunday, scan the QR code or visit the companion website at the back of this book.

Conclusion

No Perfect Pastors, Churches, or Systems

They prayed, "Lord, you know everyone's deepest thoughts and desires. Show us clearly which one you have chosen from among these two. . . ." When they cast lots, the lot fell on Matthias.

—*Acts 1:24-26*

Regardless of the appointment method to arrive at a successor (including drawing straws!), it is imperative to prepare to build the transition bridge undergirded by prayer (Acts 1:24-36). We always start our Changeover Zone workshops having an attendee read the following humorous article, titled "The Perfect Pastor," Found in many church newsletters over the years, and now even on-line. I have kept this version in my files for years. I found it from First Presbyterian Church of Tulsa in September 1980, so it has been around a while, as evidenced by the "he" referring to the pastor and the one-time popular "chain letter" movement.

Dear friends,

Results of a computerized survey indicate the perfect pastor preaches exactly 15 minutes. He condemns sin roundly, but never hurts anyone's feelings. He works from 8 a.m. until midnight, and is also the church janitor. He makes $60 a week, wears good clothes, drives a good car, buys good books, and gives about $40 a week to the poor. He is 28 years of age and has been preaching for 30 years. He is wonderfully gentle and handsome.

The perfect pastor has a burning desire to work with teenagers and spends all his time with the senior citizens. He smiles all the time with a straight face because he has a sense of humor that keeps him seriously dedicated to his work. He makes 15 calls daily to parish families, shut-ins and hospitalized, and spends all his time evangelizing the unchurched and is always in his office when needed. He always has time for meetings in the church and all its committees.

If your pastor does not measure up, simply send this letter to six other churches that are tired of their pastor too. Then bundle up your pastor and send him to the church at the top of your list. If everyone cooperates, in one week you will receive 643 pastors. One of them should be perfect.

Have faith in this letter. One church broke the chain and got its' old pastor back in less than three months. The Perfect Pastor is always in the next town over!

We can laugh at this old depiction of every church's ideal: the perfect pastor. Yet there are no perfect pastors, no perfect churches, and no perfect transition systems. For instance, many female clergy describe the systemic path to senior pastor roles in large churches as unnecessarily narrow. Women are often evaluated on proven experience; men, on perceived potential.

Our search mantra remains "not the best candidate, but the right candidate." Whether the appointment is made by the bishop and cabinet alone or in partnership with a search consultant, settling for the best candidate—who may or may not be the right candidate—can cause a transition bridge to collapse. Every pastor reaching the short list is a proven, outstanding leader. Any could be "the best" candidate, but the real task is matching the right candidate to the church's culture at the right time. The candidate must be a blessing and cultural fit for the church, regardless of ethnicity or gender.

A caution: this shouldn't sound too simple or pious. As our friend, Rev. Katie Simpson, reminds us, "The 'right fit' and 'culture match' can unintentionally become coded language." 'Fit" and "match" can reflect unconscious expectations (communication style, presence, perceived authority, family dynamics, standards) that create barriers for decision-makers.

Lovers Lane's succession team named this reality in their earliest gatherings, making an intentional commitment to acknowledge and call one another out when conversation revealed any subtle, undermining biases in search conversions. The team was blessed to have a professional HR person, Leslie Mason, as a key member. In a loving, learning way, she always kept the reality of unaware biases on the table. She also led in designing a common set of interview questions (available in the appendix) and structure that were utilized with each candidate. Throughout the search she helped create a culture in which everyone was always on the lookout for any "extra scrutiny" considerations (encompassed in the undermining assumption of women having to be exceptional to be seen as comparable).

We make it a priority to find outstanding female clergy and racially diverse clergy to become serious candidates for our largest churches. Not for "representative" considerations, but because often some of the best (and frequently hidden) clergy in our system are female pastors and ethnically diverse pastors who could bless any church and match their culture.

Case in point is Lovers Lane in Dallas. Their search started with over forty names from all over the country as possible prospects for consideration. Some of those pastors were eliminated because they lacked experience or did not match what the church was looking for, others were eliminated from consideration because their bishop did not want to lose highly talented pastors from within their respective conferences, some simply removed themselves from consideration.

Ultimately, the eight top-tier candidates identified consisted of one African American male; one Asian male; two Anglo males; and four Anglo females. The candidates who went on to become the three finalists presented by the church's SPRC/succession team to the bishop for his due diligence and subsequent appointment consisted of two Anglo female and one Anglo male. Each of the above eight pastors is an outstanding leader and demonstrates all the gifts and graces to serve well as Lovers Lane's next pastor (or most any other church, for that matter). However, because they were all so good and compelling, the church and the bishop, considering Lovers Lane's current context and needs, coalesced finally around the candidate with the most relevant experience—who happened to be the Anglo male.

Without question, Dr. Eddie Rester brought an outstanding résumé of serving very large churches; given the church's context and stated needs, Eddie's particular track record aligned closely with what the church and the bishop prioritized at that moment in time and made him a compelling match.

For many female clergy, as again Katie Simpson reminds us, "The challenge isn't a lack of calling or capability; it's the double bind of needing prior large church experience to be considered 'ready,' while having fewer pathways to gain that experience." It is our hope that United Methodism is getting closer to being more inclusive in large church leadership . . . and we are tireless advocates. Two of our coaches are top-notch female leaders who constantly teach us that in our work for leadership positions in the future we must be aware of and address the multidimensional dynamics (not just the mechanics of transition) on the part of the potential new pastor, but also that of the church itself.

For additional recommended books on pastoral transitions, scan the QR code or visit the companion website at the back of this book.

As consultants, we don't decide which pastor matches a church's culture or can lead it forward. However, all UMC clergy and laity must work diligently to improve appointment systems, especially regarding gender and ethnicity barriers.

As we work to strengthen pastoral transitions, we also work to improve ourselves as a denomination.

Great Teams Are the Magic Sauce

The fulcrum point for a great pastoral transition are the leadership teams in the church and in the conference charged with the responsibility of saying goodbye and saying hello that happens as the baton of leadership is passed from one pastor to the next over a local church's transition bridge. No modern bridge is built by one person; it takes a team. As mentioned in chapter 1, when teams believe in a great future, they can accomplish amazing things. Lovers Lane's succession team exemplified collaborative leadership, from retiring pastor Stan Copeland through each team member.

Here is how it came about from the perspective of the succession team chair, Mark Hart in a review of the process sent to us in an email:

> Our succession team comprised high-powered individuals who were highly committed to and engaged in the church. More important, they reflected all aspects of our diverse congregation. Every worshipping community, ministry, age group, and so on was represented on our team. If I'm being honest, at the beginning of our work I thought our team was too large. But the Holy Spirit must have been stirring in our midst because now, reflecting on the process, I believe having all constituents of our church represented and fully supportive of the process led to our church fully embracing Eddie when he arrived.
>
> A very important part of our process included interviews with potential candidates. Our vice-chair, Leslie Mason, led us extremely well through this process. With her professional background in executive recruiting, she established an interview struc-

ture that resulted in a consistent and thorough engagement with each candidate. Given the size of our team, it was not possible to have everyone participate in each candidate interview. Leslie designed a structure that had a small team of four to five conduct a panel-style interview with each candidate via Zoom. Further, a consistent set of topics and questions was developed to ensure a common approach. Finally, the interview team debriefed the full succession team shortly after each interview. From the candidate Zoom interviews, we invited four finalists to participate in an in-person session with the full team, presenting their vision for Lovers Lane based on the case statement developed by our succession team (with Church Difference Makers' help). By the end of this process, the team had a great sense for each candidate and would be thrilled with whomever Bishop Saenz decided to appoint.

We hope this book helps every stakeholder improve pastoral transitions. A former district superintendent in the legacy North Texas Conference, Dr. Frank Alegria, once shared the following in a cabinet devotional: "When I was a young man learning to sail, two lessons from those days have guided my life. . . . First of all, if your sails aren't set right, they flutter in the wind; they are loose; they fail to harness the momentum of the wind; you have to adjust them just a little . . . and you can feel the difference! You learn to do this through experience. Second, you constantly have to 'tack' to the left and to the right in order to move forward; it is not a straight line, but zigs and zags . . . not randomly, but always focusing on moving forward—even when at any given moment it might not seem like you are."

Progress isn't linear. Mastering the small details takes finesse, but when you do, you feel the difference. Church Difference Makers understands three key dimensions of successful pastoral transitions: (1) We value small differences that make a big difference! Shifting the culture from "we'll get through it" to "we'll grow through it" makes all the difference. We understand the little difference of intentionality makes a big difference in impact. (2) Intentionality creates significant impact. We hope you've found this book helpful and see that most guidance applies to any church, not just Lovers Lane. The difference lies not only in intentionality, but in implementation: deciding to implement it. There is a big difference from "wanting to" to "willing to."

Systems gradually solidify into their current form long after they stop flourishing. Changing systems is difficult and happens only when external conditions demand it. Without change, growth stalls.

Mark Hart has shared some kind words about us in this book, but the Lovers Lane SPRC/succession team also shared with us at Church Difference Makers their appraisal of our services, including "Suggestions for Improvements." Their list of seven suggestions included such things as:

- Engage senior staff (senior pastor, executive pastor) more, especially toward end of process. Depending on the scenario, senior staff could be critical to the transition and should be included to ensure alignment.

- And this one: "Modernize materials provided to the team; many of them seem a bit dated and would benefit from a review and modernization effort."

Ouch! But their suggestions to improve our system are what enable us to make important improvements to grow and better accomplish our mission.

In that spirit, we have written this book. We believe now is the time to make necessary adjustments in how we build bridges to the church's future. Some suggestions may sting, but they can help.

While Church Difference Makers isn't part of the official UM system, we're longtime United Methodists grateful for the bishop's and cabinet's oversight as we conduct transitions and searches in partnership with churches. We deeply value United Methodism's mutual supervision. Bishops oversee district superintendents and conference staff; district superintendents oversee pastors; pastors oversee their staff—supervision flows like a river beneath a bridge. Humble submission to proper authority is a Methodist hallmark since Wesley's time.

We understand the "super" in supervision means having a larger vision. Supervisors see from a wider perspective. This doesn't mean they're smarter or more authoritarian—only that their role requires a broader view. Even in nationwide searches, Church Difference Makers recognizes that bishops know things about candidates and local churches that we cannot see. We honor and cherish partnering with the bishop and cabinet to clarify a church's leadership needs and possibilities. All stakeholders—pastors, churches, and cabinets—must accept accountability for their roles to produce a great pastoral transition that builds a strong bridge to the church's future.

Every pastor moving to a new church wants to be like Elijah—powerfully proclaiming God's word, changing the world, calling lightning down from the sky, and ultimately being taken up to the heavens as his or her reward. But too many end up leading like Ephraim.

Ephraim is one of scripture's most fascinating characters. In bible studies over the years I have researched and taught about his story of accountability failure in Genesis 43. I have more recently observed that his story parallels many failed pastoral transitions today.

Ephraim's name reflects his prosperity and advantages, literally meaning something like, "Fruitful: A man of two pasture lands." He came from great heritage—the son of Joseph, grandson of Jacob, brother of Mannaseh And the scriptures remind us he was in the lineage that he didn't deserve from his ancestor Jacob. He enjoyed a great destiny—the prospect of becoming Israel's king. As successor, he became so influential he was often called "Israel" itself.

By today's standards, his demographics were perfect. Yet despite his advantages, his tenure was a great disappointment. He squandered his window of opportunity, which led Hosea the prophet to describe Ephraim as a man like "an unturned cake" or as more modern translations like the New King James Version say it,"a half-baked cake" (Hosea 7:8-10 NKJV; ISV). The phrase "running off with a half-baked idea" is often said to stem from this story.

This parallels pastoral transitions when a long-tenured pastor retires and a new pastor is appointed. The new pastor and baton-pass process can look excellent externally—with vision, mission, celebration, and publicity. But internally, where accountability and strategy become action, it remains underdeveloped; neither ready nor right.

We celebrate new arrangements with enthusiasm during appointment season, but without adequate transition preparation, we risk creating an Ephraim church. It looks good externally but remains half-baked internally, often ending in disappointment.

Hosea's use of the metaphor emerges from his understanding that a half-baked cake or a biscuit usually results when (1) it's cooked too hot, (2) it's cooked too low, (3) it's cooked too fast, or (4) it's cooked too slow. The balance requires right timing and intentionality—the same equilibrium needed in pastoral transitions.

Pastoral changes can't be easily scheduled. Reasons for pastoral change vary: health, death, performance, internal dynamics, external forces, and more. Still, commit to these six key components as you enter a transition:

The Six Baked-in Ingredients

- *Intentional* is the most important word in a transition,
- intentionality leads to preparation,
- preparation leads to execution,
- execution leads to accountability,
- accountability leads to results, and
- results lead to God-honoring success.

We pray churches, conferences, and pastors resist temptation and pressure to attempt pastoral transitions without all six key elements in place.

In conclusion, pastoral transitions—with or without a formal search—belong to the collective denomination, not just individual churches. How churches manage pastoral transitions shapes United Methodist culture and the broader Wesleyan tradition. God bless you, your church, and your conference in crossing the transition bridge to the great days ahead intent on reaching new people for Jesus Christ and the transformation of the world.

Notes

Chapter 2

1. Russell Contreras, "15,000 Churches Could Close This Year Amid Religious Shift in U.S.," Axios, https://www.axios.com/2025/10/03/us-churches-close-religious-shift-christians.

Chapter 4

1. "Farewell: Tending to a Soul," *A Pastor's Reflection After 28 Years of Ministry Together and What's Next*, pp. 47–50.

Chapter 8

1. Andrea Ball, "What to know about Second Baptist Church, a 98 year old megachurch being sued by its members," *Houston Chronicle*, September 29, 2025.

More Tools for Your Transition

The work of pastoral succession doesn't end with the last page of this book. We've gathered additional resources to support your church through every phase of the process.

Scan the QR code below or visit **https://bit.ly/clergysuccessionextras** to access resources including the following:

- downloadable tools and templates from the Lovers Lane succession process
- sample letters, agreements, and interview questions
- video from Lovers Lane's Passing the Baton Sunday
- a reading list for further study

Your church's transition deserves the best preparation possible. These resources are here to help you do exactly that.

https://bit.ly/clergysuccessionextras

www.ingramcontent.com/pod-product-compliance
Lightning Source LLC
La Vergne TN
LVHW031544220726
843690LV00006BA/9
9781791042400